The Value Imperative

Gerald G. Grant • Robert Collins

The Value Imperative

Harvesting Value from Your IT Initiatives

palgrave
macmillan

Gerald G. Grant
Carleton University
Ottawa, Canada

Robert Collins
Ottawa, Canada

ISBN 978-1-137-59039-8   ISBN 978-1-137-59040-4   (eBook)
DOI 10.1057/978-1-137-59040-4

Library of Congress Control Number: 2016908962

Printed on acid-free paper

This Palgrave Macmillan imprint is published by Springer Nature
The registered company is Nature America Inc. New York

For Joan and Jill

Preface

Fate brought us together in 2008, when the city of Ottawa put together a task force to look at how it was using information technology (IT). We came from very different backgrounds. One of us had been in the high-tech industry for more than 25 years working largely in the private sector. The other had been in the halls of academe. Despite this difference, we were both students of IT and how organizations used it.

As a CIO, it was painfully obvious to Rob that it was very difficult to bring technology to bear to truly affect organizations. This was not just from experience in one corporation but also through interactions with many customers visited around the world. It seemed that every CIO was struggling with the same problems. Few had had real and lasting success. Many were challenged by the inability of IT executives to be part of the strategic discussion.

As an academic researcher, Gerry had been very deliberately studying how corporations and governments invested in IT and what they got from those investments. Almost every organization understood that they needed IT to be competitive or deal with the pressures of growth with limited budgets. However, very few were satisfied with the results of the significant investments made in those technologies.

Both of us had come to the conclusion that, as an industry, we weren't very good at ensuring value was delivered from IT investments.

Modern computer-based IT has been around now for the better part of seventy years. During that time it has advanced and morphed from room-sized computers with limited capabilities at the end of the Second World War to the Internet and smartphones of today. This advance has been mind-bogglingly fast and has changed both business and everyday life around the world.

But change has not come evenly. The very pace of technological advance has tended to hide some fundamental problems that have existed from the start. These involve not just the technology, but also the management and application of that technology. The human and organizational factors have not kept pace. They have remained relatively static and, to a shocking degree, ineffective.

As a result, the IT department in any organization has somehow remained a breed apart. It is disconnected from the reality of the whole. Communication between it and the rest of the organization is fraught with misunderstanding. This leads to failures, recrimination, and, sometimes, wholesale changes that fall well short of their goals.

This can be seen when one listens, as we have, to organizations struggling to successfully deploy IT to support their efforts. The disconnect between people and groups within the organization is obvious in questions people ask us.

The organizational leadership often finds IT an enigma. Why don't we get the value from technology investments we expect? Why are projects always late, over budget, and short on functionality? Why doesn't IT deliver value? The IT leadership views the big picture through a completely different lens. What does the organization want? How do you convince executive leadership to invest in things like core IT infrastructure? Both sides are really asking, "Why don't they get it?"

IT's role in corporate governance has a checkered track record. The business asks why IT can't speak English (or French or Russian or Chinese). What, they ask, is a CIO? To whom should IT report? Wouldn't we be better off to just outsource the whole thing? The IT leadership rarely tackles these questions head on. Its focus appears to be on other things. How can we be a partner to the business? What are the best practices that others use and how do we compare? Why don't we have the CIO at the senior executive table? Why doesn't the CIO report to the CEO? Why don't the business functions participate in projects?

Often the clash comes at budget time. The executives ask, Why does it cost so much and why do you need so many people? IT asks, How do you expect us to succeed with such a small budget and so few staff? How can we control costs when those costs are driven by things outside IT's control?

Even technology is no longer a safe haven for IT. Business people ask, Why can't IT do things that their nephew can do in a few days? Why can't I use my new gadget? Why do systems fail so often? Why are they so slow? They compare them to their home Internet access and smart phone and find organizational IT wanting. IT struggles to explain the complexity of the legacy in the organization and the hype that surrounds the latest technology. The business is looking to advance, and IT appears to be trying to control and counter that.

When we first started at the City of Ottawa, the task force was pretty sure that, as a group of experienced IT professionals, we were not going to have any trouble pointing out what had gone wrong. Naturally, we turned our attention naturally to the IT department. We were surprised to discover that there was a very good group of people who were following all the appropriate practices and all the industry standards. Yet they were perceived as failing.

We spent a lot of time trying to figure out how technology should be used differently. What new advances should be adopted and what old applications should be thrown out? We kept coming back to the issue that the IT group didn't seem to be in sync with the organization. It was then that Gerry brought his academic research to bear. Cutting through the techno-babble that had come to dominate the discussion, Gerry forced the group to focus on governance.

When the time came to submit our report, we made very few recommendations about technology. We made a lot of recommendations about governance and planning. This came as a surprise to everyone. In essence, what we were saying is that the IT group was okay, but that the organization as a whole was failing. This was exactly the opposite of what had been expected.

The two of us were pleasantly surprised that, coming from such different backgrounds, we had such a common view of the problems that IT faced. After the task force was complete, we continued to discuss the challenges and failings of IT. Gerry then shared his research and ideas that became the agricultural model. Identifying the failure of the engineering model and the false lure of "alignment" that organizations sought was a major breakthrough. It meant that we had to take a different look at how investments in IT were undertaken, delivered, and measured.

Over the next several years, we continued to develop these ideas. The rigor of the academic was married to the experience of the practitioner. That juxtaposition resulted in a lot of back-and-forth. It was that give-and-take between big picture models and real-world pragmatism that, we believe, is the key to coming up with far-reaching yet realistic solutions to IT challenges.

This reached its peak when Rob took a role as a transitional CIO to change an organization's approach to IT because they felt they were failing. This provided an opportunity to put into practice what we have been preaching. This full testing of the theoretical models resulted in rounding them out in more ways than one. Not only were they more complete, but the concept of cycles became the backbone of our work.

Having tested that work, we continued to communicate more in talks and seminars. We spoke not only to IT professionals but to business professionals of all stripes. We found a special resonance with financial leaders. CFOs had come to regard IT as a giant hole in their budget that was getting bigger and bigger and one that they could not control or even understand. They latched on to the models that we provided, in some cases like a drowning man grasping a life preserver.

In all of the presentations, seminars, and discussions over coffee, one question came up again and again. Where is the book that contains all of this?

Well, here it is.

Acknowledgements

That we should focus on value is the main thesis of this book. Value creation and delivery is almost never the work of a single individual or entity. It is a cooperative and collaborative process. Indeed, we got a significant amount of value from the collaborations we had with colleagues in roundtable discussions; the opportunities to share our ideas with willing participants in seminars across North America and, in turn, to learn from their experiences; and the challenges to our ideas from both colleagues and students in the academic realm. All of this has resulted in a work that speaks to the essential issues organizations and their managers face in articulating and orchestrating value delivery from IT investments.

First, we would not be successful without the support of families, particularly, our wives Joan and Jill who have put up with us and set high standards for us to achieve. We dedicate this book to them. Special thanks to Julian Grant for applying his graphic design skills to make our diagrams look more professional. We are grateful for his patience and willingness to accommodate changes as we learned more and thought about things differently.

Every idea has a genesis. We must give special thanks to the many scholars and practitioners on whose shoulders we stand. Many have challenged conventional thinking about the way IT is viewed and managed in organizations. We are indebted to Christina Soh and M. Lynne Markus for their process view on how IT creates value in and for organizations. Their insight is foundational to our concept of value realization. Other scholars such as Claudio Ciborra challenged the neat and highly structured view of IT management that is often presented in academic and practitioner publications. They gave us the inspiration to think differently about this dynamic and multifaceted endeavor.

We would like to thank faculty, staff, and students at the Sprott School of Business at Carleton University as well as people currently and formerly at the City of Ottawa who allowed us to test our ideas on them. We are particularly grateful to a dedicated group of people who reviewed the manuscript and made us work harder to refine our ideas. Particular thanks goes to Barbara Cain for her thorough review and edit of the document. Bob Plamadon and Ken Hughes provided useful feedback on particular aspects of the work.

The book would not be possible without the support and championship of Laurie Harting, our editor at Palgrave MacMillan. She was instrumental in shepherding this project through all the processes from acceptance of the idea to publish the work to the final publication of the text.

While we acknowledge the contribution of others to this work, they are not responsible for any errors or mistakes that might appear in the text. Those are ours.

Contents

List of Figures

List of Tables

1

Business and IT Challenges for Today's Organizations

Digital information technology (IT), tools, and services are everywhere and underpin almost all aspects of modern life, whether in business, government, or society at large. Most everything we do nowadays is dependent on them. These technologies make possible new business models; new ways of connecting, collaborating, and creating; new ways of organizing and working; and indeed, new ways of socializing and entertaining. Today, large organizations such as governments and hospitals, once considered bureaucratic and inflexible, are being transformed by the innovative use of digital IT. In fact, their use is key to breaking down the traditional walls between departmental silos in both business and government. This can be seen in healthcare, where large-scale investments in IT seek to create much-needed efficiencies in healthcare service delivery, while at the same time enhancing care delivery quality and positive patient outcomes.

With all the excitement about the potential for IT to facilitate the delivery of extraordinary value, there is the sober reality that many IT-dependent projects fail to deliver their promised benefits. In the USA, the botched rollout of the Obamacare website in October 2013 is a most public present-day example of failure that can occur when business or government becomes dependent on digital business models to deliver services to customers or citizens. The difficulty with the government of Ontario's implementation of the Social Assistance Management System (SAMS) in 2014 is another prominent example. Clearly, when dealing with complex technologies, there are opportunities for failure. However, as a report by McKinsey and Company

G.G. Grant, R. Collins, *The Value Imperative*,
DOI 10.1057/978-1-137-59040-4_1

(2013)[1] confirms, many of the challenges documented are less the result of technological failures. More often, failures result from poor governance and management; inflated and unreal expectations about technology and what it can do; unrealistic timeframes for project delivery and benefit realization; and the shortage of and poor allocation of financial, human, and technological resources, among other non-technology reasons.

The Business Management Challenge

In addressing the issues faced by organizations in delivering value from IT investments, we cannot start by concentrating on the technology or focusing solely on the IT department. We must start by looking at the overall business and its strategic imperatives. What are its challenges and goals? How is it faring? Only by understanding the big picture, independent of technology, can we be properly prepared to assess how technology can be brought to bear and where best to apply it in pursuit of organizational objectives.

Enhancing the Organization's Ability to Achieve Its Strategic Objectives

Organizations, whether in the private or public sectors, must consistently deliver high-quality services that their customers or constituents are willing to pay for. If they don't, customers or constituents will go somewhere else with their money or their vote. Therefore, a key business challenge faced by executives is how to enhance their organization's ability to achieve its strategic objectives while meeting customer needs. Organizations that are deficient at setting clear objectives are likely to be less successful at generating and sustaining long-term growth. A key question though is, What are these objectives? Often, objectives are viewed from the prism of completed projects and service implementations. If the main objective of any endeavor is to get the project implemented on time and on budget, then the metrics and measures that matter will center on project delivery dynamics. However, just ensuring a product is made or a service is implemented does not guarantee use and successful adoption from customers or clients. The strategic objectives have to focus beyond the project delivery cycle to embrace the full business model. Objectives must focus on the customer or constituent to really be of substantive value.

[1] Brown, B., Sikes, J., and Willmott, P. (2013) Bullish on digital: McKinsey Global Survey results, McKinsey and Company Insights and Publications, accessed January 1, 2014 at http://www.mckinsey.com/insights/business_technology/bullish_on_digital_mckinsey_global_survey_results

In the Obamacare health insurance website debacle, for example, it seems that an inordinate amount of focus was given to the timeline for going live with the site on October 1, 2013. Consequently, important features and processes were cut and severely curtailed to meet the implementation time deadlines. While the timeline was important, if more focus had been placed on the customer experience and outcomes, different decisions might have been made about cutting functionality and curtailing important processes such as robust stress testing.

Similarly, engineers at Volkswagen[2] lost sight of what their customers value when they introduced software that allowed them to pass emissions tests in a way that did not reflect how the vehicle performed in real life. As well as angering regulators, Volkswagen lost the trust of their existing (and future) customers. The immediate costs of penalties are, by some estimates, potentially billions of dollars. The long term costs from lost sales due to the lack of focus on value perceived by customers will not be known for many years.

Market Flexibility and Operational Dexterity

Another challenge faced by organizations is market flexibility and operational dexterity. How can they be responsive to the market while at the same time being nimble in their operations? Businesses such as Dell have long thrived on their celebrated business models that embodied flexibility and dexterity. Dell's much-vaunted order-processing and supply chain management system provided significant competitive advantage for many years. However, even these models are proving to be less sustainable in highly competitive industries. More recently, Dell has had to redefine its strategy, and restructure its business and operations to survive in the IT industry. Other companies, facing similar challenges, have merged with other players (Compac and HP), been acquired by another company (Cognos by IBM), or gone out of business (Nortel Networks).

Time to Market and Cycle Times

Reducing time to market for a product or time to access and use of a service is also a challenge that organizations consistently face. Businesses must reduce the cycle time between order generation and service or product delivery if they are to survive in a dynamic and hypercompetitive world. Customers or

---

[2] Boston, W. and Sloat, S. (2015) Volkswagen emissions scandal relates to 11 million cars, The Wall Street Journal, accessed April 27, 2016 at http://www.wsj.com/articles/volkswagen-emissions-scandal-relates-to-11-million-cars-1442916906.

constituents are no longer willing to wait for long periods to get the service or product they want. They have become accustomed to getting things done almost immediately and are therefore more likely to be impatient waiting for everything to fall into place. The idea of comparing government service delivery with that of for-profit services such as Google, Amazon.com, and Facebook is now embedded in both business and political discourse. The standard for online service delivery has risen dramatically. Municipalities such as the City of Ottawa in Canada's capital are taken to task for not being able to provide the seamless experience similar to that of buying products and services through Amazon.com or eBay. Why must citizens wait, or worse yet, make several trips to a municipal office to pay a bill? Constituents now expect there to be little delay between the origination and the delivery of a service order. Anything less is a failure.

Orchestrating Dynamic Supply Chains

Products and services get delivered through an interconnected network of people and organizations. A key challenge for organizational executives is how to effectively orchestrate dynamic supply chains for products and services. Supply chains, for the most part, have long ceased to be vertically integrated into the same firm. Nowadays, there are many supply chain players and they are distributed across a wide variety of organizations in many geographic settings. Digital IT, therefore, takes on greater significance because it is essential to the flow of information across the supply chain. Without it, some supply chain arrangements are impossible. Supply chain orchestration and logistics services provided by a company such as Li and Fung of Hong Kong are legendary for their complexity and efficiency. The speed and quality of information flows within the supply chain are critical to business success.

Often people think of supply chains as only relevant to products that we buy. However, services also have supply chains. Service value chains are critical to effective service delivery. For firms and service organizations to be successful, they must optimize supply chain processes while ensuring that there is sufficient flexibility to deal with emergent issues generated in the operating environment.

Building Capabilities to Innovate and Grow

Organizations that have been successful in the past, particularly, face the issue of how to innovate and grow the organization into the future. A good example is the situation faced by Blackberry. As an innovator in the smartphone market, Research in Motion (RIM), as it was then known, gained significant market share and accolades for its ingenuity. However, it fell into the trap where its core competence became a core rigidity, a phenomenon articulated by Harvard professor Dorothy Leonard (Barton) back in 1992.[3] Leonard argued that organizations that once succeeded based on some core competence must be careful to not fall into the trap of resting on their laurels, only to find that those same competences stand in the way of being responsive to change in the environment or market. Geoffrey Moore in his book *Dealing with Darwin: How Great Companies Innovate at Every Phase of Their Evolution* talks about this issue as well. So a key business challenge for executives in organizations is how to sustain innovativeness over the long term while taking steps to exploit these innovative solutions in growing the business or service offering.

Reducing Operating Costs

Driving efficiencies in operations and reducing cost while enhancing service delivery is a conundrum for organizations. While the focus on serving the needs of customers or constituents should be paramount, organizations cannot ignore the cost of doing business. If costs escalate, the take up of products and services will decline over time. Therefore, a delicate balance must be found between cost reduction and product and service enhancement. There have been many attempts at striking this balance in both private and public sector organizations. The more recent focus on creating shared services organizations is a reflection of this. However, too much focus on reducing costs without a corresponding focus on the impacts on services can be counterproductive.

The Big Picture

Executives must acknowledge, understand, and address the wide array of business challenges organizations face, whether they are in the private or public sector. Throwing money or technology at the problem will not provide a magical fix. Leaders must actively engage in developing and applying innovative solutions to create new opportunities for sustainability and growth.

---

[3] Leonard-Barton, D. (1992) Core capabilities and core rigidities: a paradox in managing new product development, *Strategic Management Journal*, 13, 111–125.

The IT Management Challenge

One of the most significant ways of dealing with the business challenges organizations face is to apply advanced digital IT systems and services to resolve business problems and pursue business opportunities. With IT playing such a significant role in today's organizations, executives must focus their efforts on understanding and resolving the challenges encountered when applying IT to facilitate business evolution and growth. There are a number of substantive challenges that must be addressed if IT is to play an effective role is serving the organization. If enough attention is not given to these issues, failures are inevitable. Success can only come from focused and sustained efforts to deliver value from IT investments. Some of the key IT management challenges organizations face are discussed below.

Ensuring Operational Continuity Through Effective Management of Essential Digital Infrastructure

Making sure that IT works right and works all the time is the most fundamental job for any IT organization. An IT system that is not up and running cannot deliver value to the organization. Managers must ensure that the essential digital infrastructure (artefacts, systems, processes, and skills) is in place and operational. Without a robust, resilient, secure, and functioning IT infrastructure, organizations have no hope of achieving their strategic objectives. If the lights aren't on, there is no point trying to talk about other, more advanced, applications of IT in an organization. Ensuring operational and business continuity is foundational to other advanced uses of IT. Many organizations make the mistake of underinvesting in IT infrastructure in the hope that nothing bad will happen. They then expect to gain substantive business value without the corresponding investment. It's as if they believe that something magical will happen. Investments delayed for too long will always come back to haunt the organization. In one Canadian federal government department, investments in renewing the IT infrastructure kept being put off for political reasons. It seemed too expensive every time it was to be addressed. However, the systems have now deteriorated to the point where they are being "(the phrase begins with held together by duct tape". They now have to be replaced, and the bill for this is great. There is no good, cheap way to get around the work that needs to be done. If the infrastructure is not renewed, the consequences of failure will be catastrophic for the citizens. Ensuring a robust, resilient, and efficient IT infrastructure requires prescient and proactive IT portfolio management. Attention needs to be paid to designing an enterprise and IT architecture that allows for efficiencies that result from the standardization of common infrastructure.

This will facilitate the relatively easy integration of unique applications important to the success of organizational units. Too often infrastructure is allowed to become fragmented, leaving it vulnerable to failure because of gaps that develop and increase over time.

Navigating the Complex Arrays of Technology and Technological Change

Rapid and disruptive change is a constant for IT. No sooner have organizations become comfortable and competent with deploying and using a technology that it becomes obsolete. The constant change in technology is a challenge for those who must make decisions as to what technologies are important to pursue, what technologies to invest in, in what timeframe to make these investments, and how to ensure effective transition from one technological platform to the next. Currently (2015), there is growing focus on technology solutions and systems such as cloud computing, social networking, big data, and mobile computing. Each of these offer a myriad of ways to transform how organizations run their business and how they serve customers. Cloud computing arrangements offer the opportunity to provide software as a service (SaaS) such as those provided by Salesforce.com, Google, Microsoft, Oracle, and SAP. Platform as a service (PaaS) models are also possible with services such as those provided by Force.com, Google App Engine, and Microsoft Windows Azure platforms. Companies such as Rackspace, GoGrid, IBM, and SAVVIS are providers of infrastructure as a service (IaaS).

Digital social networking applications and systems have transformed the way people interact with each other in both the social and the business realm. Social networking applications such as Instagram, Twitter, Facebook, and YouTube have now been widely adopted by all types of private and public sector organizations. They are now an essential part of the arsenal of organizations intent on getting their message out to current and potential customers or constituents. Social networking, while transformative, continues to be difficult for business and public sector organizations to manage effectively. On one hand, they offer a robust and rapid way of communicating with customers and employees. They provide a rich communication platform with the ability to incorporate all types of digital media elements. On the other hand, the strength just described is also a major vulnerability. It is just as easy to provide negative and detrimental information about the organization as it is to provide positive promotional information. The easy way of sharing information means that organizational secrets can easily be shared or easily inferred from the postings of users. Organizations are challenged to navigate this perplexing situation. Some organizations take extreme measures to limit the use of social media use while others have done the opposite and embraced it completely.

Mobile computing using smartphones, tablets, notebook computers, and other devices is also presenting tremendous opportunities and challenges. The advancement in devices, particularly with smartphones and tablets, has further revolutionized the way organizations function. For example, the Ottawa Hospital, grasping the many functionalities of tablet computing, has rolled out several thousand Apple iPads to doctors and residents in their bid to "bring doctors back to the bedsides" of patients. This investment has led to widespread adoption of the technology. Plans for even greater application of mobile computing are underway. Mobile computing is not a panacea, however. The cost associated with the investment in technology is significant. New mobile infrastructure has to be built and significant effort has to be made in guaranteeing quality of service across mobile networks. This is especially crucial for applications in healthcare settings.

Organizations now face the trend where employees are opting to bring their own mobile and computing technology to work. This bring-your-own-technology (BYOT) trend presents both benefits and challenges. The benefits stem from employee flexibility, productivity, and general happiness. The costs and risks relate to the potential to lose company data and information that reside on personal devices. Organizations are taking concrete steps to manage this dichotomy. They are helped in this by substantive advances in managing mobile infrastructures and devices.

Managers dealing with the challenge of integrating emerging technologies into the business can draw on frameworks such as the Gartner Technology Hype Cycle[4]. This framework positions technology trends on a grid that plots the expectations for the technology against its eventual adoption over time. Technologies tend to get overhyped (inflated expectations) after their initial introduction to the market. However, they often descend into what Gartner calls the "trough of disillusionment" which can result in that technology losing ground and may ending up not being adopted universally. Some tech-

---

[4] Gartner Methodologies, Gartner Hype Cycle, http://www.gartner.com/technology/research/methodologies/hype-cycle.jsp

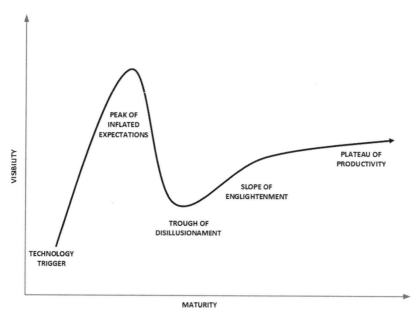

Fig. 1.1. Generic Hype Cycle

nologies survive the shakeout in the trough and begin an upward trajectory into higher productivity as time passes. The eventual productivity plateau is often much less than the initial hype. A key lesson is that technologies will be hyped to enhance the possibility of their adoption on a large scale. The question managers have to address is what aspect is hype and what is real. What are the significant affordances of the emerging technology, and how can they be applied to serve the organizational objectives (Fig. 1.1)?

There are many value-enhancing options for delivering and sourcing systems, services, and skills in the quest to generate business value using IT. Sourcing decisions are about what to make (source internally), buy (source externally), or jointly provide with others. Sourcing choice is central to achieving business success. Having great strategies, architectures, and technologies is wonderful if you choose the right provider. Choosing the wrong option for sourcing can lead to consequential failure and increased costs. The Ontario government's sourcing of its new (2014) Social Assistance Management System (SAMS) software is an example of how sourcing choice can affect organizational performance. The off-the-shelf software has been difficult to implement and use.[5]

---

[5] Vincent, D. (2015) Ontario's welfare computer glitches are not the first, The Star, Jan 25, accessed February 4, 2015 at http://www.thestar.com/news/canada/2015/01/25/ontarios-welfare-computer-

Upon launch, the software system used by 11,000 government personnel to serve over 900,000 vulnerable citizens, was plagued with data issues, defects, and delays. The Auditor General of Ontario estimated that, as of October 2015, over C$140 million in benefit calculation errors had been processed.[6] Organizations must make sourcing decisions based on their unique circumstances. There is no one best way to source IT services. It depends on the context in which the organization is operating, its strategic intent and governing philosophy, its capabilities, its experience with technology, and its maturity in business, among other considerations. To source effectively, managers need to assess and interrogate their organization's situation carefully. They should avoid succumbing to sloganeering and hype around sourcing options and instead presciently focus on what will work for the organization in that time-frame. Options thinking is paramount in these circumstances because commitments made cannot easily be reversed. Choices should not be made with only the short term in focus. They should take a medium- to long-term view of the direction that the organization wants and needs to go. The choices made should also be informed by the business and technical architecture design and direction agreed upon by organizational leaders.

Building Capabilities to Architect and Deliver Complex IT Systems and Services

The success of any business endeavor is dependent on the people brought together to design, acquire, and deliver the services. Organizations must give attention to assembling a team of experienced, innovative, and capable people who are committed to working together to design and deliver the services that will yield business value. As with sourcing, there is no one best prescription for obtaining the right capabilities. What is crucial is that executives understand that success will not happen by magic. Success comes from investing in, developing, and/or acquiring the capabilities that will make a difference. Often organizations focus on people cost, which can be significant, with a view to reducing them significantly. While such costs should be scrutinized on an ongoing basis, they should not be the "tail that wags the dog". They should be treated as one of the many considerations that go into ensuring value is delivered. Building capabilities go beyond simply hiring highly qualified people. It involves creating the atmosphere and culture where

---

glitches-are-not-the-first.html

[6] Office of the Auditor General of Ontario (2015) Annual Report: Chapter 3 - SAMS-Social Assistance Management System, accessed April 27, 2016 at http://www.auditor.on.ca/en/content/annualreports/arreports/en15/3.12en15.pdf

high-performing individuals can coalesce as a team to generate superior value for the organization. The capabilities span high-level managerial capabilities to superior operating competencies. These do not reside in individuals, but are a function of the organization. Organizations that develop and deploy advanced business routines repeatedly, are more likely to be successful over the long term. Organizations that only focus on bottom-line cost issues will likely find themselves bereft of the very capabilities needed to deliver success on an ongoing basis.

Managing the Challenges and Risks Associated with Operating on a Digital Technology Platform

The security breach experiences of Target, Sony, Home Depot, National Research Council of Canada, and many other organizations, demonstrate clearly the risks organizations face when operating on a digital technology platform. Not only are digital platforms susceptible to security and privacy breaches, the corresponding liability associated with such incidents is far-reaching and very costly both to the affected organization and to those whose information have been compromised. The cost of the security issues faced by TJX, Target, Sony, and others are in the billions of dollars. Many of these organizations are still dealing with lawsuits connected with these incidents. Some CEOs and CIOs have lost their jobs as a result. Decisions to invest or not in the necessary security and continuity protection are often "bet the company" decisions. Often these decisions are made without a full assessment of the risks and potential future costs of not making the right choice.

A New Way of Thinking About IT

We wrote this book because we want executives and other people, both business and IT, to change the way they think and talk about how IT is invested in and managed in organizations. We will introduce readers to the Agricultural Model for managing IT in organizations. With this model, we ask those involved not to think of IT from an engineering perspective but to think about IT as a farmer would.

In addition to this chapter, the book has three sections comprising twelve chapters. The first section, Chap. 2–5, introduces key concepts and ideas that are focused on changing the mindset of people in organizations about how IT should be invested in and managed.

In Chap. 2, we introduce the idea of Value Cycles. We first define what we mean by *value*. Then, drawing on the work of Michael Porter and others, we extend the thinking about value chains to that of Value Cycles. Value chains give a linear view of how organizations go about delivering value from operations. They presume that there is a customer. We propose that Value Cycles more effectively put the customer at the center of value creation activity. It keeps the focus on the customer and not on the operations. Without the customer centricity, the operations in the Value Cycle are meaningless and a costly use of resources.

In Chap. 3, we highlight the Engineering Model of thinking about IT and IT/business alignment. We suggest that the engineering way of thinking is fatally flawed and should be abandoned. It is too rigid and fails to properly account for change, which is a constant in any environment. It treats change as error. Despite its flaws, it continues to dominate the discourse on IT/business relationship. We think it should end!

Chapter 4 introduces the Agricultural Model for investing in and managing IT in organizations. We call on people in organizations to think like farmers when dealing with IT. IT investments are planned, planted, cultivated, nurtured, harvested, and renewed in an ongoing cycle. Like farmers, executives and people at all levels of the organization should focus on the ultimate aim of farming, bringing in the harvest and ensuring that it gets to market so it can satisfy the customer. Change is a given. IT farmers, like traditional farmers, need to keep a "weather eye." They should be responsive to what is happening in the environment with a focus on bringing home the harvest. Without the harvest, all efforts are in vain. Without the harvest, there will be no return on investment. We call on organizations to stop wasting time worrying about alignment and put the focus on ensuring that all efforts are focused on delivering the harvest, that is, the value that the customer or constituent is seeking. When the focus is on the harvest, alignment becomes a natural part of that journey.

In Chap. 5, we introduce The Value Realization Cycle (VRC). The VRC makes it clear that IT projects do not create ultimate business value. They create IT assets. It is the application of the assets that can create value. Value realization goes from identifying the opportunity; articulating a strategy (planning); making the investment (planting); delivering the IT asset (cultivating); ensuring that the asset is applied effectively (nurturing); getting the desired value (harvesting); and ensuring that the process is reviewed to consider the impact on strategy and future investments (renewal). The VRC emphasizes that value is created by the business, not IT! The VRC also emphasizes that value is achieved when an IT project is implemented. The work of delivering value seriously begins when the IT project goes live. A lot more investing in ensuring transformative use of the installed IT must now take place.

In the second section of the book, Chap. 6–9, we present four key considerations for ensuring that business value is delivered from IT investments. These are governance, enterprise architecture, portfolio management, and sourcing of IT systems and services.

The processes suggested by The VRC don't just happen on their own. They must be effectively governed. In Chap. 6, we show how effective governance is at the heart of value realization. It creates the framework for decision making about what opportunities and strategies to pursue, who should be involved and in what ways, what investments should be made, and how the process of value creation and delivery are monitored and measured. Governance works at all levels of the organization, not just at the board and executive levels. It has both IT and non-IT components. Effective governance entails a process of transparent and trustworthy communications with all the players involved. Without effective governance, the chance of delivering value is severely diminished.

Chapters 7 and 8 address two related issues: enterprise architecture (EA) and portfolio management. We see these both as communication tools. They are to be used to communicate what the business is trying to achieve and how the various technical and nontechnical aspects of the business can work together to deliver the value desired. EA begins with the business view at the top and is then connected downward through the data, applications, hardware, and facilities. It shows the whole and everything that is part of the whole. It communicates in both business and technical language and is meant to be understood by all, not just those who are technical. EA provides a blueprint for value realization. It is an indispensable organizational communication tool.

The complicated collection of technologies that organizations invest in can often best be understood by taking an investment portfolio view. A portfolio view suggests that there are a variety of investment options. Some IT investments are foundational and must be made if the organization is to exist and prosper. Other investments are more discretionary and can be made when possible. To have a healthy portfolio, a diverse portfolio is necessary. A portfolio view communicates value, cost, risk, and complexity. It enables decision making while communicating what is at stake.

In Chap. 9, we put the focus on sourcing for IT systems and services. Effective sourcing is critical to business value delivery. Improper sourcing decisions can lead to failure in value realization. At its heart, sourcing is about choosing the right options. Sourcing decisions should not be treated as religious declarations, insourcing versus outsourcing and propriety software versus open source, among other sourcing dichotomies. Sourcing decisions should focus on what will deliver the harvest (business value) over the medium to long term. They are shaped by what is going on in the environment. To use a farming analogy, selling the farm may make it impossible to plant new fields in the future.

Section three of the book, Chap. 10–12, turns the focus to how to measure whether value indeed has been delivered and whether there has been effective return on the investments made. Chapter 10 argues that if you cannot measure it, you cannot manage it. Measures are not necessarily monetary or quantitative. There can be qualitative measures as well. We argue here that everything can, and must, be measured.

Return on investment (ROI) is the ultimate definition of the harvest. We argue this position in Chap. 11. Since investing in IT is one among many options for allocating organizational resources, ROI is the only means to effectively compare alternatives to a particular investment. ROI is not only expressed as the financial increase gained by investing in IT; it may also be expressed in terms of risk and costs avoided. Sticking with the status quo also has ROI implications.

We discuss the role of leadership, including that of the CIO, in Chap. 12. We see leadership of the chief executive officer (CEO), chief financial officer (CFO), chief information officer (CIO), and other business unit leaders as pivotal to organizations delivering value from IT investments. CIOs need to be both business and technical leaders of their organizations. These two orientations must be expertly managed if the CIO is to be effective. We discuss the challenges that these two accountabilities bring and make suggestions as to how the CIO can be most effective in the roles. We also discuss the roles of other leaders, particularly those of the CEO and CFO. Their involvement and decision making is central to organizational success.

We conclude the book by challenging business and IT people to focus on the harvest (the business value that customers seek). If we take our eyes off the harvest, we will engage in a lot of activities that, at the end of the day, will be meaningless. By focusing on the harvest, we will avoid flushing our resources down a deep dark hole, something that many organizations are doing on an ongoing basis. Let's think differently about IT!

Discussion Questions

1. What are the major business challenges facing your organization (a) at this moment, (b) in the next year, (c) in the longer term?
2. What strategies should your organization apply to address the challenges faced?
3. Which technological challenge is most significant for your organization?
4. What steps should your organization take in addressing these technological challenges?

2

The Value Cycle

Organizations invest in digital information technologies (IT) to create value for the organization and its stakeholders. They do not (and should not) do it to be up-to-date with the latest technology or to create more interesting work for IT professionals. Shareholders, customers, citizens, and donors put money into organizations to get some value out of them. This is a vital truth that must be understood by people in IT as well as those in other parts of the organization. For business value to be derived from IT investment, it must be possible to clearly articulate what that value is. It cannot be a vague concept that is not measurable. Value must be measurable and must also be measured in practice. Only then can there be accountability for the results as well as learning for continuous improvement. For our purposes, *value is the agreed-upon benefit to be derived from applying IT to support the delivery of outcomes customers are willing to pay for or fund*. (Customers, in this instance, is used as a generic term to refer to clients, constituents, donors, voters, and other stakeholders for whom value is being created and delivered.) Profit resulting from commercial activity by business firms may be one measure of business value. Other measures could include outstanding public service delivery (such as clear roads in winter, faster ambulance or fire response times) by a municipal government, significant reduction in medication errors in a hospital, or increase in the number of meals served by a not-for-profit or charitable organization. If value is not perceived by customers, they will not pay for or fund it over the long term.

© The Editor(s) (if applicable) and The Author(s) 2016
G.G. Grant, R. Collins, *The Value Imperative*,
DOI 10.1057/978-1-137-59040-4_2

Business value is a contested idea in that organizational stakeholders may have different views of what constitutes value. It is also possible that stakeholders may agree on a value proposition that may be difficult or impossible to achieve in practice. Sometimes it may be possible to realize value that is superior to what was projected. While these are all true, it should be clear that once the organization agrees on the value they expect to be delivered, then IT investment decisions, whether at the strategic, tactical, or operational levels, must be judged by their contribution to delivering that desired value. By clearly articulating the business value sought, the organization provides a point around which all stakeholders can coalesce. Research and practice have demonstrated over time that the value desired and the value realized can often diverge. Realized value is what the organization is able to achieve in practice. Some may view realized value as failure, that is, not achieving the expected value. However, realized value may either fall short of or exceed expectations. The realized value may be viewed as the battle-tested outcome and may indeed be more realistic than the preimplementation conceptualized value. In measuring value then, attention must be paid not only to expected value but to realized value as well. The reason for divergence must be thoroughly interrogated and analyzed to determine if the gap between the expected and realized value is realistic or problematic.

Customers are central to the value question. It seems obvious, but it bears repeating, that before making any investment in IT, executives in organizations must understand who their customers are, what they want from the organization, and how the organization makes money fulfilling their demands. Businesses, governments, and other public and private sector organizations exist and become legitimate because they deliver value that their customers want. So if businesses fail to deliver what their customers want, the customer will walk away—physically, financially, and emotionally. When they do, it is difficult to get them back. If a government fails to deliver value to its constituents, it will lose trust and legitimacy in their eyes. If a not-for-profit organization loses its customer focus, it will soon be seen as illegitimate in the eyes of both donors and clients.

With the vast amounts being spent on deploying digital IT-based solutions, it seems incredible how often and how spectacularly seemingly well-conceived and well-funded projects fail to deliver the value sought. The disastrous rollout of the US healthcare.gov website when it was launched on October 1, 2013, is a case in point. The failure of the website provides a teachable example as to what organizations do wrong when they lose sight of what's key to value delivery, their customers. When the Obamacare team found that the rollout of the site faced significant challenges before launch date, all the decisions, about what functionality to include or cut and how the information could be accessed, made consumers a victim rather than a customer when they tried to sign up for health insurance. Key customer-friendly applications such as the ability to browse plans before signing up were left out. This led to widespread frustration and bad publicity. Lost in all the techno-babble and recriminations was the fact that what the consumer really wanted was to be covered by health insurance as soon as possible without much difficulty. They wanted to know what their options were before making a decision to sign up or not. While the task of providing the service to customers across the USA was always going to be challenging and complex, the website was a means to that end, not the end itself. It took a massive intervention to refocus the efforts on the consumer, rather than some date for go-live. Now when you go to www.healthcare.gov, you will find a website that is more customer-centric. The improvements in the site came about when the customer once again became the focus. While the website has been repaired, that damage to the program's reputation remains. As with any major technical failure, fixing the technology is the easy part. Restoring the credibility of the organization is much more difficult, if not impossible.

Value desired does not automatically translate into value realized. However good the description, actual value delivery results from effective, on-the-ground execution in practice. Getting value in reality is not always a straight-forward process. Achieving the result sought often involves missteps, setbacks, improvizations, and a lot of learning-by-doing. A relentless focus on planned and realized value from the customer perspective is essential to success. Organizations must know how the customer desire will be served in practice and how the organization may sustainably deliver that value over time. Organizations need business models that work. History is full of examples of organizations that started with a great idea but lacked a sustainable business model that could deliver value repeatedly over time. The business model describes how the organization generates value. Making decisions to invest in IT without a sustainable business model is a ludicrous waste of resources. IT is not an end in itself and must serve the business goals and objectives. We believe that success in generating business value through IT investments is predicated on a good and thorough understanding of the organization's Value Cycle. A lack of understanding will exacerbate unplanned missteps, disconnects, and setbacks.

Value Chains and Value Cycles: Key Roles of Information and Information Technology

Harvard professor Michael Porter[1] popularized the notion of value chains to highlight the key processes that any business must execute to generate value. The traditional value chain is viewed as a linear process with activities such as inbound logistics, operations, outbound logistics, marketing and sales, and service. These are the primary activities. A set of support activities (administration and infrastructure, human capital management, procurement, and product and technology development) are critical to ensuring value is created and delivered. The value derived from the activities in the value chain depends on the efficiency and effectiveness of information flows and process execution along the chain. The more efficient and effective the connections between the activities, the larger the margin that will be generated.

While this model has been widely adopted and has been influential in business circles, this linear view of value creation implies that that there is a customer who may be targeted for marketing, sales, and service. The customer, though, is not seen to be central to the process. The customer is assumed to be available and involved. However, many of the activities in this linear model can and often are executed without customer involvement. There is a certain "if we build it they will come" quality about this arrangement. As we have seen from many examples in industry, customers do not always come.

We argue that, instead of looking at value creation in a linear way, like a chain, the process should be viewed as a cycle with the customer at the center. In this way, customer requirements and outcomes become central to all activities in the Value Cycle. This is important because at no time should the organization lose sight of the customer and his or her requirements. At the end of the day, if the customer fails to be satisfied with what is produced, all the activities in the Value Cycle will have been done for nothing.

Value Cycles describe a set of interconnected processes. They begin with a set of primary activities that must be executed if any value is going to be delivered. These are supported by a set of other activities that facilitate the accomplishment of the core activities. All activities in the organization are further supported by a set of infrastructural services, systems, and facilities that support efficient and effective process execution. In a product provisioning context, efficient and effective information exchange becomes central to value generation. The role of the IT function within the business is to provision the

---

[1] Porter, M. (1985). *Competitive Advantage: Creating and Sustaining Superior Performance*. New York: Simon and Schuster.

IT infrastructure and supporting applications that will optimize business processes and streamline information exchange. To the extent that this is done, IT becomes a crucial link in the Value Cycle. It forms the platform from which a wide variety of value-enhancing applications can be launched (Fig. 2.1).

Each process in the Value Cycle can be performed within the firm or be procured as services from other firms. Some firms, like Samsung Electronics, have a web of integrated services that are internal to the corporation ranging from inbound logistics to manufacturing to sales and marketing. Other firms like Apple outsource their manufacturing and logistics to organizations such as Foxconn. Sales and marketing are done either directly through their own stores or through partner organizations such as telecommunication services

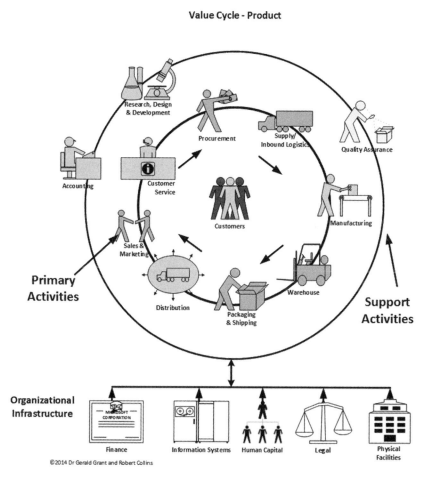

Fig. 2.1. Value Cycle—products

companies. Each process in the Value Cycle can become the anchor point for a firm's business. However, at the end of the day, it is what the customer will pay for that will determine what gets produced, distributed, and sold. This fact makes it critical for business managers to ensure that they do not focus solely on what IT wants to achieve to the detriment of what the business needs to achieve to remain solvent and profitable. If the business is not profitable, it will soon disappear. Then there will be no IT to make decisions about.

Flows and Asymmetry of Information in the Value Cycle

The role of IT investments in the Value Cycle is to increase efficient and effective information flows and reduce information asymmetry. All transactions in the Value Cycle depend on the effective flow and management of data, information, and knowledge between each of the processes. If the flow of data and information is disrupted or defective, the extent and quality of service delivered will be defective as well. The distortion in flow results in information asymmetry and can occur at any point in the Value Cycle. Information asymmetry is a big problem in Value Chains and also in Value Cycles. What this means is there are often disconnects between the information that one element in the Value Cycle is producing and what the connecting element requires to carry out its tasks. For example, if the wrong specifications are sent from the design shop to the manufacturing shop, the wrong product could be manufactured. Similarly, in a service situation such as the US Healthcare. gov website case, asymmetries arose when information from applications did not pass in a timely and correct manner to insurance providers. This led to demand for changes to the program. In a healthcare setting, information asymmetry often occurs when information captured at one point of care is not accessible to service providers at another point of care. Missing important information such as medication interaction can lead to catastrophic outcomes for patients. Combating asymmetric flows of information is an ongoing challenge. If not addressed, these asymmetries can add substantial and unnecessary cost to organizational effort. They reduce business value. Making changes to correct or reduce asymmetries can be costly. This is why it is important that organizations work to break down silos between units that must collaborate to deliver value. Walls between organizational units that create asymmetry will increase both direct and indirect costs. These costs could include losing customers because of poor products or service offerings.

By articulating and documenting their Value Cycles, organizations can identify and measure the potential or real effects of information asymmetry between processes in the Value Cycle. It forces them to think about and assess the possible points for production or service disruption so that they can develop strategies to mitigate their occurrence. Failure to anticipate, measure, and correct the disruptive elements in the Value Cycle will increase the risk of system failure, and ultimately result in the reduction or total loss of business value.

Value Cycle for Services

Since many of today's organizations are service organizations, they do not have the same processes as a product-producing entity. Value Cycles for services illustrate key differences that must be considered by service-provisioning organizations. Services are somewhat different from products because services are produced and consumed simultaneously. While the service infrastructure may be in place, the service only gets produced when the customer accesses it. It means that if a service is not available when and how the customer requires it, that opportunity is lost forever. Other service opportunities might arise in the future, but the one missed cannot be recaptured. The inability of prospective customers to log on to a website (as was the case with healthcare.gov) or the inability to access the inflight entertainment system on a long flight are examples of this. Services are also different because they are often coproduced with providers. They are often intangible, that is, they exist only through the interaction of the customer and the provider. It means then that satisfaction with the service is highly dependent on the performance of the provider in the moment of access.

Service delivery is often highly dependent on IT, as is the case for many online services such as those provided by retail banking and ecommerce sites (for example, Scotiabank.com and Amazon.com) or public sector sites (for example, www.healthcare.gov and www.nyc.gov). Service delivery in an online environment is built on a service platform and infrastructure comprising informational, human, technical, and physical resources. A weak or defective service platform and infrastructure will lead to poor service delivery. We see this in the initial rollout of the healthcare.gov website. The service delivery platform was defective. Its architecture made it difficult to scale when demands exceeded capacity. There were also significant disconnects in the information architecture such that people had difficulty signing up, and there were problems with information transfer to insurance companies. This led to widespread anger about the whole program. By contrast, organizations such as Amazon.com, eBay, and various retail banking and airline reservation systems have robust digital service delivery platforms. These have allowed them to serve millions of customers at scale across many demand cycles. While they are not immune from failure, they tend to be more resilient and responsive (Fig. 2.2).

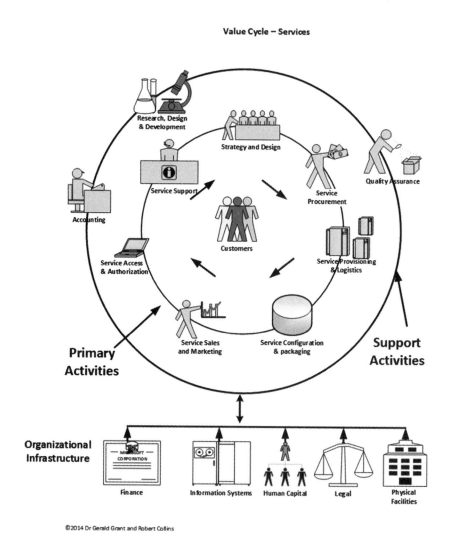

©2014 Dr Gerald Grant and Robert Collins

Fig. 2.2 Value Cycle—services

Keeping the Focus on the Customer

Many IT and business people spend a lot of time and money trying to align business and IT. The problem with the whole idea of alignment is that it is based on the premise that there are two separate entities trying to come together. If most of the effort in determining how to effectively deliver business value is spent talking about business-IT alignment, the organization should right away know that it is in trouble. When you focus on the customer and what it takes to deliver a product or service that is high quality, timely, and safe, alignment of all aspects of the organization should be a natural outcome of that process. Often, then, the question is not whether there is alignment or not. It is more about what the focus of organizational effort is.

Business Value, the Cornerstone of IT Investment

As we will see in the following chapters, business value is the cornerstone and key rallying point for investment decisions, project delivery, asset maintenance, and the ultimate and effective alignment of organizational activities (including those of the IT department). Customer-centric value generation is the key to long-term growth and sustainability of any enterprise. It is central to effective and sustained alignment of all organizational activities and investment decisions. When decision makers focus on business value, questions about alignment will no longer preoccupy them. Their decisions will be shaped by efforts to generate and reap the business value produced. Alignment will be a natural consequence of that focus.

In the next chapter, we discuss the *Engineering Model* for managing IT investments in organizations. We show the inadequacies of the engineering view in addressing the core challenges faced by leaders making decisions about IT investments. The notion of business-IT alignment is a central pillar of the Engineering Model. We see this eternal pursuit of business-IT alignment as chasing a mirage. We address how real alignment may occur by proposing a new approach, *the Agricultural Model*, to be discussed in Chap. 4.

Discussion Questions

1. Identify and describe the primary and support processes in your organization's Value Cycle.
2. What are the potential asymmetries and disruptions that may arise in the execution of the Value Cycle?

3. What steps should your organization take to mitigate the risks that the asymmetries identified pose?
4. What is the potential for making the current Value Cycle more efficient and effective? What would you change? What would you not change?
5. Who is at the center of your organization's Value Cycle?
6. Who else could be at the center of that Value Cycle? Who do you think should be there?
7. What does the person at the center of your Value Cycle expect from your organization? How would they articulate that?
8. How is the person at the center of your Value Cycle manifested in your IT investments?

3

The Engineering Model of Business-IT Alignment

In 1999, I became chief information officer (CIO) of a major software company. Having risen through the ranks of the Products Division, I knew that I needed to learn a lot. So I dove into anything that could broaden my horizons. An obvious starting point was magazines aimed at the CIO. Almost all of these talked about the Holy Grail—business-IT alignment

If IT and Business could just be aligned then everything would be fine. It was this missing element, experts explained, that was at the root of all of the problems. This made sense to me just as it did to every CIO I met at conferences. We all agreed that we needed alignment with the business. There was only one problem—we hadn't found anyone who had successfully achieved this.

Twelve years later, I was sitting in a lobby waiting for a meeting. I noticed a copy of a magazine with CIO in its title and picked it up to fill my time. Its cover story—We need Business-IT Alignment! In twelve years, the story had not changed one iota. If this really is the key to success, then how is it that, as an industry, it has not progressed in any meaningful fashion? -- Rob Collins

Information Technology (IT) organizations have not been unaware of their challenges in communicating effectively with others. Recognizing that there is a problem, IT departments have sought alignment with the rest of the organization. As noted above, this drive for alignment has been ongoing for decades. It is regularly cited as one of the major goals of IT organizations. Yet the search for alignment has not brought about the desired goals. In this chapter, we will look at why alignment and the ubiquitous Engineering Model for investment in IT has failed us.

© The Editor(s) (if applicable) and The Author(s) 2016
G.G. Grant, R. Collins, *The Value Imperative*,
DOI 10.1057/978-1-137-59040-4_3

What Is Business-IT Alignment?

For almost three decades, business executives, consultants, and researchers have been talking about strategic alignment between the business and IT. Yet, we seem to be nowhere nearer to achieving such alignment despite the heroic efforts of business and IT practitioners. Alignment is said to occur when there is congruence between what the business wants to achieve (its strategy) and how IT may serve that strategy. In that scenario, the efforts of business and IT are synchronized as a well-engineered machine delivering extraordinary value to the business.

Though everyone talks about business-IT alignment, do we really have an understanding of what it means in practice? More often than not, it is taken as a given without any effort to analyze the concept. Let's break this down into its component parts. What do we mean by business, IT, and alignment?

Business is the raison d'être for any organization. The organization exists to achieve some purpose and has some broad means of doing so. The stakeholders, be they shareholders, voters, or donors, are focused on achieving some end through their investment in this organization.

IT, in this context, refers most often to the IT organization. This is the department that is responsible for developing and maintaining the information and communications technology infrastructure. Technology aside, this is a group of people with specialized skills whose job it is to support the rest of the organization.

Immediately, something should jump out at you. Why is IT, as part of the organization, defined separately from business, which is the entire organization? Is it somehow distinct from the rest of the organization? Does IT matter more than other components?

IT is a service and support function. The organization does not exist to allow IT to function. IT exists to allow the organization to function, hopefully more effectively and efficiently. There are other functions in a business with a similar role. The obvious counterparts are Human Resources (HR) and Finance.

Part of the challenge is that IT is a relatively new function. Whereas Finance is using processes developed in the fifteenth century, IT has been part of organizations for less than a century. During those decades, the technology has changed fundamentally many times. As such, IT has not settled into a familiar and accepted role within the typical organization. It is still viewed as an outsider, both by itself and by other parts of the organization. (Perhaps the Medicis agonized similarly over double-entry bookkeeping as a discipline in 1415.)

Now, what of alignment? If parts of the organization have a common and complete understanding of each other, is there a need to create alignment? No. But this is not the case with IT in almost all organizations. IT does not understand the business and the business does not understand IT. So the two must be brought together.

Most often, this is expected to be accomplished by regularly occurring planning and strategy exercises. For a majority of organizations, this is an offshoot of the budgeting process. The organization plans its strategy. Then each function goes off and plans its part in achieving the strategy. At some point, these various parts meet with IT to arrange for technology to support their plans. In truly enlightened organizations, this may be done with all functions at the same time. But more often than not, it is done independently for each function.

Having met and set plans, the business functions and IT go their separate ways. If they are aligned, it is expected that they can proceed in this fashion and arrive at the desired destination in the future, in harmony. Everyone can tell stories about how, as events unfold, the harmony dissipates. Work is then done to correct alignment. And at the next point, the process is repeated again. Alignment is something that happens as an exception. It may occur at specific points in time, but is rarely maintained (Fig. 3.1).

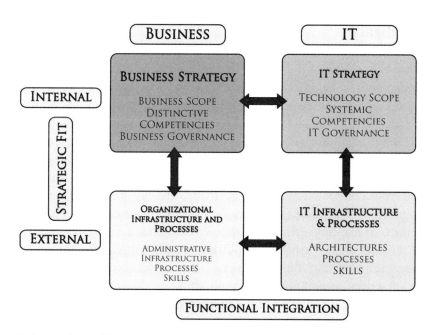

Fig. 3.1. Business-IT strategic alignment model

It also happens, or fails to happen, at various levels of the organization. Alignment may be reached when the budget is settled at the top of the organization. Then IT starts projects, brings in project managers, and starts working to a project plan. The assumption, that the project started with alignment and therefore will stay aligned, is not realized in practice. Project plans, carried out by middle and junior levels of the organization, do not have the alignment that started at the executive levels. Projects do not track alignment. They track functionality, time, resources, and money. Over time, this focus on project variables replaces the goals and alignment. By completion, the original objectives may have been forgotten completely.

Finally, there is a curious concept embedded in the very question of IT-Business Alignment. The implication is that IT is equivalent to business. It is a peer. Many consulting companies promote this idea, trying to help CIOs put their organizations on a par with other business functions. Is this reasonable? IT, like HR and Finance, provides services and support to the business. Like the others, it does have a mandate for some level of control (security, continuity) over business activities. But it does not directly deliver business value as certain core business functions such as manufacturing, sales, or service. It exists solely to make the other functions (including HR and Finance) more effective. In essence, IT, for its own sake, does not matter.

The Mirage

IT often fails to deliver on its promise because IT and business managers consistently adopt an engineering approach to delivering IT systems and services. IT is seen as an engineering discipline. For decades, IT professionals have used engineering titles and terminology and aspired to be equivalents of those with professional designations.

The persistence of the strategic alignment concept among IT practitioners, consultants, and researchers is a testament to the prominence of the engineering perspective. It results in the acceptance of a mechanistic view of alignment that presumes—as in the realm of engineering, building construction, or manufacturing—an ideal that is known, standardized, measurable, and achievable. Alignment outcomes can be predicted and achieved through learning and the refinement of standard routines and practices. These practices, once known, are replicable and customizable to suit various circumstances. While acknowledging some level of dynamism, deviations are contained, accounted for, and circumscribed in arriving at the desired solution.

A typical IT project is most often equated with a construction project. Requirements are identified at the beginning. A solution is defined, reviewed, and refined. A project plan is laid down with budgets and timelines. Staff are assigned and work is undertaken. Every effort is made to ensure that once work begins, there will be no change.

Change is the enemy of projects. It is identified as error. If there is a change, it is because something has been done wrong. The users did not define the requirements correctly. The designer did not do a thorough job. Outside forces conspired to undermine the brilliantly defined plan. Good project managers go to great lengths to find and stamp out change.

When change must happen, it is a major exercise. The project is halted. Change orders are drawn up. The effort to ensure that, this time, we get it all right is repeated. Then, with a new schedule and different parameters, the project is resumed. Change remains the enemy. It is costly, embarrassing, and not to be tolerated.

IT as Construction

When a building is being built, engineers use this same approach. At the start, they identify what the building is for—housing, business, manufacturing, and other uses. Then they put together plans that are approved by the client. Contractors are hired and the building is built. Even with the best of efforts, schedules are often missed. But rarely do they build the completely wrong building or does it fall down after they are finished.

The reputation of IT projects has not been as positive. Far too often, the result is less than was expected (both in functionality and quality), at a greater cost, and later than needed. Why does IT have such a poor track record compared to construction companies when they are using essentially the same techniques?

When a construction company builds a building, there are a very limited number of variables, and deviations are easily resolved in advance. If a building is to be an office, how many people must it hold? What kind of offices are needed? What are the weather conditions? All of this can be known in advance. When people move into those offices, they will do, essentially, the same office work they did before, but in better surroundings more supportive of their efforts. Outside of their commute, their business processes will not significantly change.

IT projects have almost nothing in common with this. In almost every case where this is a significant investment in IT, it is to bring about process change, not support existing processes. An upgrade of an email system may make minor improvements to existing processes that do not cause major change. But a new Enterprise Resource Planning (ERP) system or a shift from direct to online sales implements radical change to an organization. This has no direct comparison to the engineering of a clearly defined construction project.

The true value of IT is its ability to facilitate such transformational change. Attempting to use a methodology where change is considered error, to bring about massive change is clearly not going to work. And, as an industry, we have decades of failed projects to prove it.

The Spiral

This fallacy of a perfectly engineered ideal creates a spiral that takes projects out of control. At the beginning, every effort is made to define the project so that there will be no unanswered questions before work begins. Only in this way can we be sure to stick to a rigid schedule and budget. Everything is signed off by the business and IT.

As soon as the users see the first glimpse of the new system, things often begin to fall apart. This phenomenon has been perfectly illustrated by the SAMS project being implemented by the Government of Ontario. In late 2014/early 2015, the Ontario government rolled out a new system, called SAMS—Social Assistance Management System—to support social services in the province. The implementation was so disastrous that it made headlines throughout the province and was the subject of call-in shows and editorials. The primary goal of the new system was to collect better data on the distribution of social assistance. This was driven by the provincial government.

However, the administration of social assistance in Ontario is done by municipalities. Interface with recipients is handled by staff employed by cities and towns with funding coming from the province. The application, developed by the province, focused solely on the goals of those in the back office. The workers on the front end had no say and were not effectively consulted.

When the system went live, without a phased rollout or parallel testing due to schedule pressures, it destroyed business processes across the province. The neediest people in the community were put at risk when their support workers could no longer manage them through the new system. The province was forced to pick up the tab, reported at $5 million for overtime and extra training for the municipalities.

The *Toronto Star*[1] reported that the program cost $242 million for development and $21 million for additional staff costs (overtime, training, new hires to replace workers who quit or went on stress leave) of which $11 million had been budgeted. Failures in the system resulted in overpayments of $20 million. In March, an additional $5 million had to be allocated to clean up the mess.

There were many problems with the SAMS project. But the most obvious is that it failed to focus on the citizens receiving the service (the person in the center of the Value Cycle). To compound that problem, it failed to understand the processes that led to that service being delivered (the various rings in the Value Cycle around the person at the center). The objective for those developing the system was better data. But the objective (or harvest) for those using the system was support to the community. By completely missing the Value Cycle, the project was doomed to failure regardless of the quality of project management and technology involved.

There is almost always a watershed when the users first engage with the new technology. It is most often at this point that the business begins to think about the details of process change that will be necessary. This is true no matter how well-meaning, capable, and committed the business is to the change. Transformational change is so dramatic that the full understanding of it requires interaction between the management, users, process designers, and technology staff on an ongoing basis. At each interaction, something will be learned that will refine, or even question, the basis on which the project was planned.

At this point, good project managers step in to correct the situation. They push back on "scope creep". If the users insist, they do proper change requests and alter the schedule and budget accordingly. This usually meets with dismay from senior management who have already set a budget and expect to reap the rewards of the new system within a certain timeframe. The project team then compromises. Some functionality is dropped to reduce the time and budget. This satisfies the project plan but puts the expected benefits in doubt. That is too often not considered as, by now, the focus has become solely on time and money.

This process is repeated, often because the functionality dropped earlier is discovered to be essential and has to be added back in. Other functionality is dropped in its place. In many cases, supporting processes are the first to go by

---

[1] http://www.thestar.com/news/canada/2015/03/19/ontario-pours-another-5-million-into-problem-plagued-welfare-computer-system.html

the wayside as the focus narrows and the clock ticks. Training and post-go-live support usually fall victim to this.

IT projects that deny the reality of change, classifying it as error, are reaching for the false promise of the nonexistent oasis, a mirage, seeming to exist in vivid, lifelike color, but in reality, actually nonexistent. As with the mirage in the desert, the expectation of a truly satisfying, thirst-quenching outcome disappears into a bowl of sun-baked sand when the target is approached.

The Holistic Model

This problem has not gone unrecognized. Various models have been developed to try to account for the problems commonly found in the engineering approach to IT.

Most commonly, managers seek a Holistic Model. This is an attempt to go beyond the occasional alignment points between IT and business. Instead of going separate ways after achieving alignment, this model sees business and IT staying, and working, together as a holistic effort rather than parallel. The Holistic Model has shown great promise in bringing problems forward earlier when there is more time and tolerance to deal with them. What the Holistic Model, and other alternatives, have not done is overcome the spiral. Projects and systems are not better as a result. This is because they are still following an Engineering Model at heart. They still regard change as error that should have been addressed at some earlier point.

The Holistic Model has identified that there is a problem, but has not correctly identified the problem. Its conclusion is that IT and business need to work more closely together over time. This is true. But it misses the need to manage change as part of the project. Without that correction, all Engineering-based Models are treating a symptom and not the underlying fatal flaw.

IT Plans

While organizations want IT to better align to the business, IT is struggling to communicate that it has requirements which must also be addressed. IT is responsible for an infrastructure upon which most organizations are completely dependent. This is the natural focus of IT, which if left to its own devices would consume its entire budget and resources.

Like any infrastructure of buildings, roads, pipes, and so forth, the IT infrastructure of networks, communications tools, and applications must be maintained. Industry analysts advocate that 60%–70% of IT's budget should be applied here. This is difficult for businesses to understand when they see this large expense with no additional value being created.

This is exacerbated by the rapid change in technology. Where roads and sewers are expected to last decades, technology components rarely last as long as five years. Worse, within three years, many components are technically obsolete. The need to keep up to date as well as to keep functioning puts heavy demand on IT departments.

These needs create further stress on the business-IT alignment. As well as addressing the failures of the Engineering Model, there is a lack of common ground and understanding, and IT leaders must bring forward large and costly budget pressures that show very little return on what is perceived as new investment.

There Is Hope

This engineering motif is problematic when addressing the issue of IT's role in business strategy. In totality, a goal of alignment can have a profoundly negative effect on the realization of IT benefit by reinforcing the separation of the "Business" and "IT" agendas. While recognizing that IT and related infrastructures have significantly engineered components and processes, thinking about alignment in engineering terms may be limiting at best and fatal at worst as current business and IT orthodoxies are constantly being challenged by new realities. Therefore, focusing on alignment in these terms may lead to organizations' failure to embrace the capabilities and functionality embodied in newer technologies, systems, and processes.

So long as IT professionals strive for the mirage of business-IT alignment, things will not change. Only by acknowledging the deficiency of the Engineering Model, can we expect better results. But what will replace that Engineering Model?

In the next chapter, we propose and discuss the ***Agricultural Model*** for managing IT investments in organizations. We contrast the Agricultural Model with the Engineering Model, which is the dominant way of thinking about managing IT in organizations. The Agricultural Model represents a dynamic and improvisational approach to managing IT that accounts for environmental and organizational change. Change is acknowledged and embraced.

Discussion Questions

1. What is your view of the idea of business-IT alignment? How do you see this being achieved?
2. What is your response to the criticisms raised about business-IT alignment as an engineering construct?
3. Discuss the extent to which the Engineering Model of business-IT alignment is practiced in your organization. What are its effects?
4. What steps should be taken to ensure better alignment between business and IT?

4

The Agricultural Model

Earlier in my career I fully embraced the notion of strategic business-IT alignment. Theoretically, it seemed like a reasonable idea. With so many practitioners and academics writing and talking about the need to align business and IT I joined the bandwagon. I taught it, researched it, and published a paper based on the idea of strategic alignment. However, as I continued to see organizations struggle to achieve alignment I began to question the way the concept was operationalized. The messiness and fluidity of events and activities in the process of acquiring, deploying, and using IT in organizations defied the neat, orderly, and episodic engineering ideal captured in the business-IT alignment motif. Exposure to the ideas of people like Claudio Ciborra, Bruno Latour, and others crystalized my own thinking about how organizations may effectively acquire, deploy, and use IT. I came to the realization that achieving business-IT alignment as popularly articulated in both business and academic settings was a false dream, a mirage. A new approach was needed. The idea of approaching the process of acquiring, deploying, and using IT from an agricultural perspective began to germinate. I had previous experience overseeing the management of a large commercial farm and had some exposure to the vagaries of delivering a profitable harvest. The farming metaphor seemed to provide a better explanation for managing IT. I first articulated these ideas in an editorial in the European Journal of Information Systems (EJIS)[1] -- Gerald Grant

In the previous chapter, we outlined the challenges with adopting an engineering mindset when addressing the issue of business-IT (information tech-

---

[1] Grant, G. G. (2010) Editorial: Reconceptualizing the concept of business and IT alignment: from engineering to agriculture, *European Journal of Information Systems*, 19, pp. 619–624.

nology) alignment, suggesting that this approach is limited and problematic in the longer term. In this chapter we suggest a different way of understanding how organizations can effectively realize business value from their investments in IT. We argue that leaders and managers should adopt an agricultural perspective. This is an alternative to the engineering view that has served us so poorly.

When thinking about delivering business value from IT investments, we suggest that executives look to agri-business for insights. Agri-businesses make money (in some cases a great deal of money) while dealing with a considerable amount of uncertainty. They cannot fully predict the weather. Will it rain? Enough? Too much? What will the harvest be like in other parts of the world that compete for the same markets? Will there be challenges such as insects or crop diseases? None of these things are fully known when the season starts. And yet, these businesses continue to thrive. Not every year is a success, but the vast majority are. How does an entire industry deal with the uncertainty and change of such a model, and what can we learn from it?

The main difference between the agricultural and engineering models is the attitude toward "change" and adaptability. In the Engineering Model, change is error. It is to be avoided and eliminated. This is, as has been said in the previous chapter, the unrealistic flaw that undermines this model. In the agricultural motif, change is expected. It is something to anticipate and manage; not something to be avoided. Change is embraced when the agricultural perspective is adopted.

The Agricultural Model also takes a much broader ecological view of the environment in which the organization operates. It clearly adopts a general systems perspective where all systems are interconnected and affect each other. Where the Engineering Model is often isolated and focused on specific technical systems or projects, the Agricultural Model recognizes that everything is interrelated and interconnected.

The IT Farm

The IT farm is composed of fields; technical and physical infrastructure; the intellectual property; and the human, financial, and other resources available to it. The resources are finite and decisions have to be made as to how best to use them. On the farm, the fields represent the opportunities for developing and producing a crop that can eventually be harvested and sold. Similarly, organizations have fields of opportunity where investments of IT and other business resources provide the bases for exploiting business opportunities. A farmer's decision to plant a certain crop in a field is akin to a decision by organizational executives to make a particular IT investment. Once the decision is made and the field is planted, the options for using that particular field are very limited (one could always plough it in early and do something else, a very unlikely occurrence) or nonexistent. The same can be said for IT investments. Once made, they are difficult and costly to reverse.

Fields often have different types of crops growing in them. The crops may have different origins. Some may have been germinated on-site, others purchased or acquired through other means. Similarly, an organization may have different IT fields with different systems in them. Some of these systems may have been developed by the organization itself. Others, such as Enterprise Resource Planning (ERP) systems, may have been purchased as off-the-shelf software. Some systems might have been acquired to bring in best practices of an industry to the organization. Others may have been implemented to support practices that make one organization different than others. Still others may have come in as part of a merger or acquisition—essentially increasing the size, and complexity, of the IT farm.

Fields do not operate in isolation of the farm infrastructure. To be effective and productive, they must be supported by the irrigation systems, tractors, physical buildings (barns, grain silos, etc.), and other infrastructural investments that provide common services to all fields. Organizations also must invest in infrastructure that provides common services across the entire entity. IT infrastructure comprises all the physical and technical components (networks, servers, data storage, enterprise applications, and access technologies), and technical staff, systems, and processes that can be readily accessed by any IT application or service.

Differences exist between the various crops in the various fields. Not all crops have the same lifecycle and they do not mature at the same time. In IT terms, this means that not all systems require the same intervention at the same time or follow the same cycles. This is a good thing. Having systems with different temporal requirements and cycles allow organizations to manage the operational peaks and lulls in a more balanced way.

IT fields come in different sizes. Some are very large (e.g., ERP [enterprise resource planning] systems) while others are small (e.g., decision support for specific departments). Size must not be confused with importance, though. In agriculture, a large crop, like corn, may take up many acres but produce a lower overall return on investment (ROI) because of the market dynamics. A small crop, like an organic vegetable, may produce much more revenue per acre. Similarly in IT, smaller systems may well support critical business functions even though they require far fewer IT resources than larger systems used by many departments.

Such a variety of crops requires different cultivation techniques. The work to grow and harvest a large corn crop to be sold to an industrial buyer is going to be quite different from that required to produce an organic vegetable crop to be sold at local markets. It should be possible, however, to produce both crops without creating duplicate infrastructures. The same should be the case with IT in organizations. It should be possible to leverage established IT infrastructures when developing different types of IT systems.

The quality of the crops will differ as well. In a commodity market such as livestock feed, the quality may only need to meet a minimum standard. Whereas in a competitive market like fruit sold directly to consumers, producers must compete on quality and may therefore be able to command a greater price. IT systems that are differentiators for organizations must meet a higher standard than those that are merely industry-standard processes. The effort expended and the investment made for these should differ in direct relationship to the value to the organization. For example, making the ERP system better with more bells and whistles that do not materially affect the success of the organization is a waste of investment. There's no point making the corn beautiful if it's all going to end up as cattle feed.

At the same time, aesthetics do matter. In agriculture, we know that oddly shaped tomatoes do not command the same price in a supermarket as perfectly round ones. This is true despite the fact that the two tomatoes may taste the same. The comparison in IT is the usability and compatibility of systems to the users' expectations. While two systems may do the job equally well, the one that fits with the users' expectations and is easiest to use within their business model is going to produce a better result faster than the one that forces users to adapt without offering them any additional value.

Alignment in the Agricultural Model

In the Engineering Model, business-IT alignment is the goal that has eluded organizations. The idea that various parts of the organization come together to agree on things and then go their separate ways has not worked. Continued focus on getting better alignment within this model has proved less fruitful while consuming a tremendous amount of organizational resources. With the Agricultural Model, alignment is not the primary goal. Achieving *the **harvest*** is the goal. The harvest is the expected value, defined by the business, that the customer is willing to pay for or fund. It is the return expected from an investment. The harvest is expressed in business terms (e.g., increased revenue), not in technology terms (e.g., transaction throughput). While alignment is not the central goal in the Agricultural Model, alignment is more likely to occur when everyone is focused on the central goal of delivering the harvest.

This requires IT to speak to the organization in its business terms. Too often IT forces the user communities to speak about technology or, in some cases, the users drive the technology discussion without a full understanding of the implications. Speaking about technology rather than value, inevitably leads organizational personnel to make the error of focusing on that technology, losing sight of the return that was the whole point of the investment.

In the Agricultural Model, the coming together of the various functions to achieve a result is an evolutionary and ongoing exercise. It is not something that happens once in a while with parties coming together briefly for joint sessions and then going their separate ways soon after. It is dynamic, anticipatory, and reactive. Expecting change, the team must interact frequently to consider how to deal with emerging issues. With the returns (or harvest) as their common guide, there is a motivation and basis to work together.

Change Is Not Failure

Unlike with the Engineering Model, which treats change as error, the Agricultural Model embraces change. Change can come from within a project, for example, because of incorrect or incomplete requirements, wrong assumptions, or overly optimistic schedules. These are the changes project managers are used to dealing with. But change may also come from outside. Market conditions, such as an economic downturn, may change the expected returns. Other systems or projects may have an impact that was not expected. Competitors may act in a way that must be countered. Continuing on as if these things did not happen is foolish, and yet all too common.

By embracing change, organizational managers look for these internal and external forces. It is the job of the team not to avoid change but to evaluate and manage it. Identifying those changes is a vital skill (the weather eye) that must be cultivated and rewarded.

Using the harvest as a guide and metric against which to manage change provides common ground that keeps all parts of the organization aligned. It provides a goal that allows people to understand the need for change and a measure by which to assess alternatives and choose new options.

Consider this oversimplified example: A project is designed to support the sales teams working in retail stores. Let us say that there will be 1,000,000 transactions per year that currently cost $5 per transaction. The new systems will reduce this to $4, saving $1,000,000 per year. The cost to produce the system will be $1,500,000. Over three years, the harvest will be $1,500,000 (3 × $1,000,000–$1,500,000). During development, the organization discovers that a competitor is taking market share by selling online rather than through stores. The organization quickly reacts and also sells online, stabilizing revenue and retaining customers. However, this reduces in-store transactions to one half of what they were. That means the return for the retail project is now only $500,000 per year. The ROI now is $0. In the Engineering Model, the project might be delivered on time and on budget and the IT team might celebrate the success. But it was not a success, as it produced no ROI. In the Agricultural Model, a good weather eye would catch this problem and either adjust the project to improve ROI or cancel to eliminate the expense that produced no results.

The Agricultural Life Cycle

The Agricultural Model can best be understood as a life cycle of activities and processes that begin with *setting a strategic direction* and ending with delivering the harvest and assessing the impact of the activities undertaken. A good farmer does not simply go out and begin planting a field. Delivering a bountiful harvest usually begins with preparation and planning. Once a direction is set and strategic choices are made, planting can begin. *Planting* represents the first step in creating the asset. For the asset to reach a level of maturity and quality such that it can be released into production, it must be *cultivated*. While the asset might be technically of good quality and is ready for deployment, it may face issues relating to organizational fit for use. The quality asset must therefore be *nurtured* to ensure that it can be successfully used to deliver the value expected. Successful and effective use should lead to the delivery of the *harvest*. No one aspect of this process cycle is sufficient on its own to deliver the harvest.

The Agricultural Model requires the entire organization to participate in the value creation and delivery activities across the cycle, not just IT. There is work belonging to IT and there is work that is for other parts of the organization. No project or system can succeed if the processes are kept separate in functional silos. To get the expected harvest (value), the whole system must work together.

The model is applicable both to new projects and to the systems already in place. Where the Engineering Model only accounts for specific projects in isolation, the Agricultural Model accounts for systems through their entire life cycle and does so in context of the environment in which they exist. Organizations spend up to 70 % of their IT budget on their legacy systems and processes. Any good model must account for this large share of ongoing expense. We explain each process in detail below. We begin with the harvest.

The Harvest

The harvest is the business value delivered following investment in IT systems and processes. It is the articulated value that the organization seeks to achieve and represents what customers are willing to pay for and fund. It must be expressed in business terms that would make sense to a customer. It is different from IT value and cannot be expressed as technical metrics (throughput, server capacity, etc.). At its best, the harvest is defined by a measure that can be related back to the organizational strategy.

Most importantly, the harvest is not the resulting technology. A new server is not the harvest. The profit generated by enabling more customers to order online using the new server would be the harvest. If one only talks about a server, then the outcome will only be a server. But if the focus is on a value metric such as profitability, various possibilities open up. Some might be technical—a faster network rather than a new server. Others might be an issue of sourcing—putting the order system in the cloud rather than buying hardware. Others may be nontechnical—reducing the cost of the product to increase profitability. When the focus is on the harvest, all of these are in play. When the focus is on the schedule to deliver a new server, the server delivery will be the key outcome.

The harvest is not always measured in monetary values, though this is most common. It may be measured in time to service a customer or availability of data for decision support, or other nonfinancial measures. It is always a business value that can be recognized by any organizational stakeholder and one that they are willing to pay for or fund.

The harvest is the single most important concept in the Agricultural Model. At the beginning of any project, there is some assessment of the expected outcome or return to be achieved. Often, with the Engineering Model, this very rationale for a project becomes lost because of the inordinate focus on project management and its metrics (cost, time, resource, and schedule). Rarely, if ever, does the team step back and consider how they are doing relative to that original goal. Too often, the strategic objective is not even measured after the project is completed.

When a decision is made on changes to a project, it should be done relative to the original goal, the expected harvest. When functionality is reduced, it does not just affect the schedule. What is the impact on the resulting value? When training is cut to save a few dollars, is there consideration of how that will affect the realization of the value originally sought? If the time to deliver is extended, does this have any impact on the harvest, which may have been based on assumptions of delivery at a certain point in a business cycle? The harvest should be the primary consideration and focus of every decision from the time an investment decision is made until the time that the resulting system is taken out of service.

The quality of the harvest is affected by a number of factors. On the farm, the quality of the soil, the other crops in the fields, the environment, and the effort put in by the farmer will affect the resulting harvest. In IT, the quality of data, infrastructure, integration, and business processes will affect the quality of the harvest. These should be understood up front so that realistic expectations can be set before any effort is undertaken. Also, we should consider what quality of harvest is necessary. That will avoid investing more than is necessary and incurring higher opportunity costs.

Thinking about the harvest in these terms speaks to the issue of sustainability over time. The harvest is rarely a one-time event. Systems that go into production for years are more like orchards than fields of wheat. An orchard must be managed for the long term. Initially, as the trees grow, the harvest may be small. Over time, it is likely to become more bountiful. As trees age, their productivity may reduce until they become more valuable as firewood than producers of fruit. So it is with technology. At first implementation, the harvest will likely be smaller as people learn to use the systems and the bugs are worked out. Often organizations go through a period of shakedown and disillusionment. This should be expected, and efforts should focus on managing through that phase to keep it as brief as possible (see Cultivation and Nurturing below). With greater use in the normal business process, the outcome is expected to be greater. Then, over time, current systems may become less relevant as processes change, market conditions shift, and they no longer integrate with newer technology. At some point, the cost of maintaining the system can be greater than the value created. This "negative harvest" is a sure sign that new investment or culling is needed.

It is important to understand when to measure the harvest. The use of the system within the cycle of business processes is analogous to the ripeness of a crop. Harvesting too early reduces quality. Measuring results before they truly affect the desired measure produces an inaccurate understanding of the value created.

Planting

On the farm, planting is putting the seed (or sapling, etc.) into the ground. In IT, it is the initial phase of bringing some potentially useful IT system or service into being. Just because acquisition of the system or technology has started does not mean the value sought will be achieved. Like a seed when it is planted needs tending, new IT systems and services will only produce value when applied to the relevant business processes that can generate the value (harvest) expected.

The Engineering Model emphasizes the planting phase. Great rigor, applying a variety of well-known techniques (from systems development life cycle [SDLC] to prototyping to agile systems development methods), is put into requirements definition and system development or acquisition processes. The focus is getting the right system developed for the right price, delivered at the right time. There is often little focus on the expected harvest.

This is not to say that the planting isn't important. It is obviously vital. If the seed isn't planted, there will be no harvest, no matter how hard one tries. The planting is essential but not sufficient. It is one step in the overall process. Poorly planted seed will likely yield a poor harvest. This is the same for poorly specified and developed IT systems. Such poor systems will make achieving the value expectations difficult if not impossible. That is why it is essential to emphasize the importance and relevance of all the tools and disciplines that have grown up around systems analysis and design, systems development and acquisition methodologies, and project management. These continue to be necessary and important in the Agricultural Model. The big difference between the engineering and agricultural models is that in the Engineering Model, the planting becomes the central focus. In the Agricultural Model, the planting is a necessary step in the cycle for delivering value.

Cultivation

Cultivation is the effort to take what is planted and ensure that it grows into something that will produce the desired harvest. In agriculture, this is the weeding, watering, pest management, and other related activities. If a farmer plants a crop but then ignores it, he can expect a poor harvest, if any at all. Similarly, if a system is developed and then left unmaintained, it will certainly not magically produce the business value expected.

In the IT world, cultivation focuses on what is necessary to make the asset effective. This can include anything internal and external to the asset that influences its performance. Is there enough network bandwidth? Is there appropriate connectivity with other systems? Do we have enough server and storage capacity? All of these things will have been defined to build the asset. However, no system ever performs exactly as expected at first. It is vital to take the time, and make the measurements, to ensure that the new asset is performing as required to achieve the harvest. Note that this is not the same as saying it is performing as designed. By focusing on the harvest, we bring into play the unknowns that may not have been in the specifications but that, nevertheless, affect the return the asset can be used to provide.

A good example of issues needing attention after asset creation is quality of data. Poor-quality data may be preventing a system from being effective, reducing productivity, and upsetting users. Efforts may be necessary to address legacy data issues in order to ensure that a newly created asset achieves expectations. This effort may involve no change to the asset created, but is nonetheless vital to reaping the harvest.

Another challenge to be considered during cultivation is duplication. If multiple fields are planted with the same crop, but there is a market for only half that much, then there is waste. This effectively reduces the value of the harvest by half. On the IT farm, this phenomenon commonly manifests itself in duplicate systems, applications, and services. Having different users performing the same functions in different applications with different data sources is a sure ticket to a low-quality harvest and long-term maintenance costs that are unnecessary. Such an approach creates a bad environment for other systems needing to integrate.

What is needed is careful, adroit, and very intentional action to mature an asset into something that is of the required quality, a necessary step in the Value Realization Cycle (VRC).

Nurturing

While cultivation focuses on the asset created by the planting, nurturing focuses on the environment and user community into which the asset is applied. Nurturing is doing similar work for the business side of any system as opposed to the technical aspects. We want to make sure that the cultivated asset is effective in the business environment.

Nurturing starts with the business users' involvement right at the beginning of any decision to invest in a system. When the user community is on board and committed to reaping the harvest, even a system with problems has a good chance of succeeding. When the user community is resistant to the change, even the best system can fail. If no one wants to buy lima beans, there's little rationale in planting them.

One of the most common sources of change, and friction, in any project is when the new tool is first applied to the business process—be they existing or new. Inevitably, as users interact with the new technology, they discover problems in matching it to their work. Too often this results in a fight between the business and IT as to whether the requirements are right. That is because the Engineering Model requires you to take all unknowns out of the equation before you start.

That is simply impossible. It is only reasonable to expect that when the system is first applied, things will be learned that require some adjustment. Sometimes that adjustment is in the technology; other times in the business process. Regardless, making that adjustment is vital to achieving the harvest. By keeping the focus on the harvest and assessing issues in that light, the system and users can be nurtured to success. Being prepared for change at this time in the schedule is good management and must be part of every deployment plan.

To do this, it is necessary to have the team in place to work with the users when they first begin to use the new system. Too often the team is disbanded at the end of planting and the users are left to their own devices putting extensive pressure on a smaller support team. This is like abandoning the process in the depths of what Gartner calls the trough of disillusionment (see Chap. 1). For success in exiting the trough, it is necessary for the support team to interact with the users, ensuring that problems are addressed and solved expeditiously. It is not enough to wait for problems to be reported. To ensure a quality harvest, the team (both technical and business) should be out there in the user community seeing the system in use and working proactively and improvisationally on the issues that may affect achieving the harvest.

Substantial process transformation is vital at this stage. As well, proper training of the users in new business processes and the technology supporting those processes is mandatory. Doing this is costly and time-consuming but necessary. It cannot be left to chance or the whim of managers. It must be a well-thought-out part of the overall strategy. This is not the place to cut costs as is common in practice. A well-functioning asset is left unused because the necessary training, change management, and incentives are not put in place to drive adroit and effective use.

Renewal

As said earlier, very few systems are implemented as a one-shot harvest. The vast majority must produce a harvest year after year. It is as important to apply the Agricultural Model to assessing the ongoing harvest of existing systems as it is to focus on the harvest for new ones.

What crops did well? Which of the systems are functioning well and producing a quality harvest? This requires us to measure the harvest made possible by these systems. If they're doing well, do we see any threat to that performance in the future?

What crops were disappointing? These are the systems that failed to produce the expected harvest. Why are they underperforming? Is the asset fundamentally flawed (planting)? Is there something wrong in the technical environment (cultivating)? Is there a problem with the users or business processes (nurturing)? Is it environmental (infrastructure)? What actions can or should be taken to restore the harvest? Is it time to reallocate these resources to something else and retire this system (plant another crop)? It is vitally important for organizations to periodically assess their portfolio of IT assets to ensure that they are producing value (a subject to be discussed in more detail later).

What are our opportunity costs? What wasn't planted that could have been? Is there still satisfaction that the right decisions were made at the outset? What new crops are out there that should be considered for planting? In IT terms, are the right technologies being used? Are they current? What new technologies are emerging that should get more attention?

Are common problems manifesting themselves across multiple systems? If this is the case, there might be infrastructure issues. As a farmer must keep the irrigation, tractors, and equipment running, so must IT keep the networks, servers, and various underlying technology primed and effective. Assessing the harvest impact on each of the systems can provide the business case for making further technology investments that would benefit all functions.

The Agricultural Model Is Less Predetermined

No one would suggest that a project should begin without a plan of how to get it done and how much it would cost. Good planning and project management remain vital. But these tools must not become straightjackets that prevent success. Following the Agricultural Model means being prepared to react to change as well as proactively look for change in order to be able to act quickly and early. The goal is not the schedule. The goal is the harvest.

Change is not error, as it is perceived by those applying the Engineering Model. Change is a fact. The ability to manage change is the key to success. The incorporation of change and the requirement to manage it creates opportunities for innovative and entrepreneurial behavior. Indeed, it requires them. When an original assumption or environmental change has thrown a project off course, opportunities to correct the divergence should be sought. With the harvest as a guide, alternative courses of action can be planned. This means that rigidity must be replaced by flexibility.

In farming, the harvest can be bountiful, exceeding expectations, normal (as expected), or falling below expectations. The same can be said for the value delivered following IT investments. Just because the harvest falls below expectations does not mean that there is an outright failure. In fact, delivering a harvest at all could be seen as an extraordinary feat in the context of adverse environmental conditions. Too often, IT managers feel the wrath of their counterparts in the business because of a perception that expectations have not been met. While they are justified in their criticisms in some circumstances, executives and managers should not lose sight of the fact that value delivery may fall below expectations in the first phase of implementation. They should avoid "throwing the baby out with the bath water". Even projects considered failures initially can be considered outstanding successes in another timeframe. This was the case with Hershey's implementation of its complex ERP and distribution system in the early 2000s. Hershey suffered an almost catastrophic system failure shortly after project go-live that cost the company hundreds of millions of dollars in lost business. However, once the problems were resolved, the project was deemed a success for the business.

Organizations, because of guidance resulting from focusing on the harvest, may be better able to determine when to abandon a project that will not deliver any value. Cutting projects loose early is a good thing because continued funding of bad projects only wastes valuable resources. If, at the earliest stages, a farmer determines that the crop he or she had planted will not deliver a return, it is best to plough the field in rather than waste resources bringing the mature crop to harvest. What would be the point of cultivating, nurturing, and harvesting the plant if at the end no one will buy it? The same goes for IT projects. Kill them early if they will not deliver value in the end. Don't waste valuable resources keeping a project going. Focusing on the harvest allows organizations to cut losses early and reduce financial and business risk.

Acknowledging Limitations

A Limited Acreage

On a farm, there are a limited number of acres to utilize for growing farm produce. A decision to plant a certain crop, say corn, on some of those acres means that the farmer is making a decision NOT to plant something else on those acres. Once planted with corn, it cannot also be used for wheat. Similarly in IT, if resources (technology, staff, and money) that are in limited supply are applied to a specific system, those same resources cannot be used to do something else. An option has been exercised. The opportunity cost for that investment decision must be accepted.

This does not apply solely to the IT department. Any organization, or part thereof, can only consume so much change at any given time. If a major new system for the finance department is deployed, that department will have to dedicate resources and revamp processes to gain the benefits of this system. Trying to implement a new business intelligence system for financial data at the same time creates a likelihood that both projects would fail. While IT may be able to bring different resources to bear on two such simultaneous projects, the finance department does not have the ability to support that much work. It is most likely that a few key resources would be vital to both projects and cannot be spread that thin without negative implications.

There is a cost aspect to this that is often not considered. Deciding what to do (e.g., plant corn) is deciding what not to do (e.g., plant wheat). When the cost of planting corn is considered, should not the lost opportunity cost of having foregone wheat be considered as well? When presenting the investment cost of any system, the cost of not pursuing a valuable option should be presented as well. This way, organizations will have the full picture, and opportunities for second-guessing decisions will be reduced.

Infrastructure

Infrastructure has its limitations. Planting more crops that will outstrip the irrigation capacity of the current system will be problematic. Can the irrigation system live up to the demands? Similarly, developing and deploying systems that outstrip the capacity of prevailing IT infrastructure will create problems for the organization. Putting more people on a network without increasing bandwidth will lead to slow response and limit the capacity to accomplish the job.

Sunk Costs

Finally, sunk cost must be recognized. Once a crop has been planted in a field, plowing it under to plant something else means that no harvest will be achieved. No one has the luxury of unlimited resources or budgets. Sunk costs are not limited to a specific system. Every organization has its legacy. That legacy is of great value. Developing a new system that does not exploit or provide compatibility with that legacy can be an expensive decision. Considering the whole farm when planting a new crop will ensure that compatibility is taken into account. Very few systems in today's world exist on their own. At some point, the data must come together with that of others to provide a whole-organization view.

Shifting to the Agricultural Model

The shift from engineering to Agricultural Model is not a small one. The Agricultural Model requires organizations to deal with the big issues that the Engineering Model hides. Where engineering presents the mirage of knowing everything in advance and having a guaranteed schedule, the Agricultural Model recognizes that this is not possible and brings the uncertainty of change directly into the management of IT. How can an IT department make this shift?

The first step is for the IT leadership to start talking in business terms and expressing themselves in ways that focus on measurable results that make sense to all the organizational stakeholders. The harvest creates a target that is comprehensible to user departments, management, executives, IT, Finance, Human Resources, and so forth. Because this focus is common to all, the harvest creates the alignment that is elusive to the Engineering Model and does so in a way that persists over the life of any system(s). That change puts a measurable outcome in place that encourages all to participate where the technical jargon of the past repelled them.

As things proceed, it is vital to keep the focus on the harvest. There is a temptation to fall back to old models and terminology. To lose focus on the harvest is to lose alignment and risk everything. The IT leadership and business leaders desiring change brought about by technology must be consistent, always starting and ending discussions with the harvest and using it to provide the basis for all decision making.

It is equally necessary to give up on the mirage. This means admitting that everything cannot be known in advance. In place of false certainty, it is necessary to communicate how a "weather eye" will be used to forecast and anticipate change and how change management will become a bedrock principle of technology projects and systems support.

This change is unsettling to people, as they feel that admitting to uncertainty makes it less likely that organizations will make investments in technology. This is wrong for two reasons. First, after half a century of IT projects disappointing more often than they succeed, no one actually believes it when the CIO pronounces what the final date and cost will be. By admitting what everyone knows and hitting the issue head-on, leadership can gain credibility. Second, the commitment to managing change, measured against the harvest, can allay the greatest fears of CEOs (chief executive officers) and CFOs (chief financial officers)—the runaway IT project. IT projects are notoriously hard to kill, clinging to the mirage of almost being there. By committing to the organizational leadership that a project will regularly assess the situation with an open mind and a focus on the expected ROI, it becomes more likely that a failed project can be stopped early, reducing costs and reassigning resources. This risk reduction makes it easier for leaders to make investments knowing that they can cut their losses.

This does not preclude the need for good planning, disciplined management, and solid methodology. What it does is give these virtues a framework to fit into the big picture of organizational strategy and investment decisions.

How Do You Use the Agricultural Model?

The harvest should be the basis of any conversation about a potential technology or existing system. The chief information officer (CIO) should understand the harvest that is expected and the harvest that is received of every application for which they are responsible.

The harvest creates alignment. Ensuring, before anything else, that the user community and IT have a common understanding of the harvest is essential. From that common objective comes the alignment that we seek. No matter how troublesome matters become, it can always be addressed by returning to the harvest and examining the issue in light of that goal. That removes all references to personal preference, technology, or even politics. If a problem cannot be seen to have an impact on the harvest then it is not a problem and should not be consuming resources. If a technology is not positively affecting the harvest then it has no place in the solution.

The harvest is also the basis of governance. The goal of any project is not to implement technology but to solve a business problem. The role of governance is equally to ensure that the business problem is being solved and staying solved. By focusing higher levels of governance on this rather than on the details of schedules and features, projects stand a much better chance of succeeding or, where appropriate, being stopped before they consume too many resources.

Success of a project is also far more likely if the full cycle of planting, cultivation, nurturing, harvesting, and renewal are the focus rather than just the planting. First, this model ensures that these various phases are considered right from the start and that they are all seen as equally important to success. Throughout the project, from planting to harvest, having the right people in place with the right focus and the common goal is something that can be planned and managed. Attempts to take shortcuts can be assessed in their likelihood of affecting the final harvest rather than just the asset creation schedule.

The Agricultural Model puts IT at a more senior, and business, level than project management. (Remember, project management is still very important. It is just not the be-all and end-all.) When the CIO and IT can show a full understanding of the organization and the consequences of various technical situations in terms that make sense to the rest of the organization, they are in a position to provide leadership.

Very important to IT, renewal is a phase that deals directly with some of the greatest challenges they face. Being able to articulate how infrastructure influences multiple systems and their various harvests is an effective means to get organizations to invest in technology that they would otherwise not want to hear about. Being able to explain how older systems no longer deliver a real harvest is a means to manage a portfolio and stop it from growing out of control.

That idea of portfolio management, which we will discuss more in a later chapter, is vital. Various systems do not exist in isolation. There is an entire IT farm with its own ecosystem and culture. Changes and problems in one place have an impact throughout. The Agricultural Model provides a framework in which to understand and communicate this.

Put simply, the Agricultural Model is one that takes the alignment created by understanding value and applies it to everything IT does. This ensures that alignment is maintained and strengthened and brings IT and other departments together in the most effective manner possible.

Culture Change

There is no question that this represents a significant, and positive, change of culture from the Engineering Model. Like any significant change, moving to the Agricultural Model is an exercise in change management. It does not happen overnight, although the focus on value can happen very quickly. Introducing the new concepts, training, and testing their application should be a cornerstone of such a shift.

It must also be remembered that culture is not limited to IT. It must be embraced by the organization as a whole. An evolutionary approach can yield better results than revolution. While the concepts should be introduced to the whole organization, the focus of efforts can be initially directed at specific projects and departments, preferably those who will take on this change with a positive spirit. Then the details can be extended to other departments with the lessons learned and, hopefully, a successful project to show its potential.

Expect to take at least a year to get full buy-in and understanding of the Agricultural Model, and expect it to be several years before it has completely replaced the old culture.

Don't try to boil the ocean.

The Agricultural Model Is All About Value

The Agricultural Model goes far beyond the limited vision of the Engineering Model. It takes into account the entire environment. It deals with the reality that change happens. It incorporates good management and methodology and provides a framework for contributing to higher-level decisions. It creates lasting alignment through its focus on the *harvest*. It deals with all the aspects needed to make systems successful—planting, cultivating, nurturing, and harvesting. In the renewal phase it not only assesses ongoing projects but also the use of all the limited resources across the entire organization. It acknowledges reality and reduces risk.

It requires new skills—a weather eye, flexibility, and entrepreneurship. It requires discipline and measurement to make the assessments of the harvest. The next chapters will go into more detail on these concepts and explain tools and techniques that can be applied to implement the Agricultural Model in any organization.

By focusing on the outcome, rather than merely the delivery of a piece of technology, the Agricultural Model makes success far more likely. Whereas the Engineering Model focuses solely on the planting (creation of the asset), the agricultural view looks to success factors in the cultivation (ensuring the technology is effective, not just meeting specs), nurturing (ensuring that the people are effective with the technology), harvesting (ensuring and measuring that value is achieved) and renewal (ensuring the long-term delivery of value) phases of any technical solution.

Discussion Questions

1. What are the core ideas of the Agricultural Model?
2. How would you apply these ideas to decision making about IT investments in your organization?
3. Use the model to assess one IT investment decision and its roll-out in the organization.
4. How would decisions made be similar or different if the traditional engineering view is used?
5. How would you sell the use of the Agricultural Model in your organization?
6. What would have to change for the ideas to be adopted?

5

The Value Realization Cycle

In Chap. 4, we introduced a new way of looking at information technology (IT) investments—the Agricultural Model. We strongly believe that this model is a more realistic representation of the world in which IT is being applied to the challenges of any organization. In this chapter, we will bring together the Agricultural Model with the Value Cycle, introduced in Chap. 2, to show how IT investments are turned into real business value through the Value Realization Cycle (VRC).

Business and IT executives continue to make the mistake of equating investment in creating an IT asset with delivering business value to the organization. Both research and practice, time and again, demonstrate that this is not the case. When a project team successfully delivers an IT asset to the organization, such as a fully functioning SAP system or an electronic medical record system in a hospital, it does not mean that the organization will get the value expected. All they have done is to create a well-developed and sophisticated IT asset. There is no direct link between investment in an IT asset and ultimate business value outcomes. Investment in IT is a necessary, but not sufficient, condition for achieving IT-related business value. Business value results when an appropriate strategy is agreed upon; the right choice of IT investment is made from among a portfolio of possible investments; a well-developed and fully operational IT asset is created and put in production; the appropriate institutional, process, and people changes are implemented to create business impacts; and those impacts are effectively harvested to deliver the value sought by the organization. All of this is possible only if organizational leaders and members are able to govern and navigate through

© The Editor(s) (if applicable) and The Author(s) 2016
G.G. Grant, R. Collins, *The Value Imperative*,
DOI 10.1057/978-1-137-59040-4_5

Fig. 5.1   The Value Realization Cycle (VRC)

the constantly evolving and dynamic environment in which the organization operates.

One way of understanding how organizations can realize business value outcomes is through the VRC in Fig. 5.1 above.[1] The VRC is a model that represents the series of activities and related processes, each necessary but not individually sufficient, that collectively are essential to value realization. It covers the key aspects that must be considered in the planning phases and that subsequently must be enacted in practice to ensure effective identification, acquisition, deployment, and use of IT investments.

What the VRC tells organization leaders and members is that value realization is a fully engaged process that goes beyond any single area of focus. It requires intense and continuous oversight and cannot be left to "IT people" alone. Leaders must pay careful attention so that activities and decisions are focused on value at each stage of the cycle. If organizational leaders and members take their eye off value realization, resources (human, financial, physical, and temporal) will be expended on initiatives that have no significance to

---

[1] The model is draws on Soh, C. and Markus, M. L. (1995) How IT Creates Business Value: a Process Theory Synthesis. In Ariav, G. et al. (eds.) Proceedings of the 16th International Conference on Information Systems, December 10–13, Amsterdam, Netherlands; and Marshall, P., Mckay, J., and Prananto, A. 2005 Business Value Creation from IT Investments: Towards a Process Theory of IT Governance, *Australasian Journal of Information Systems*, 12(2), 192–206. The Value Realization Cycle (VRC) specifically puts the customer at the centre of the cycle emphasizing the pivotal roles customers play in the ultimate determination of value.

value realization. This is like pouring scarce resources down the drain. Once expended, they cannot be recovered for something more profitable in the future. For example, many organizations have invested in large-scale enterprise resource planning (ERP) systems that were not necessary for the size of business they were installed in. The legacy of this type of investment is long-term commitment to expensive upgrade paths and maintenance fees that deliver little value.

What customers value and are willing to pay for or fund are at the heart of the VRC. By focusing on customers and the value they seek, organizations will not become fixated on one aspect of the Value Cycle or another but will be responsive to the dynamism in the environment that may shift what customers value over time. By keeping an eye on what customers value, organizations will at least know which activities and decisions are appropriate and which are not.

Components of the Value Realization Cycle (VRC)

Strategy

One of the key benefits of the VRC, in relation to IT investments, is to clearly show where and how IT assets fit into an organization's strategy. Although the VRC should not be treated as entirely prescriptive and deterministic, it suggests that eventual value realization will best occur in the context of a well-articulated strategic direction. Investing in and creating IT assets without a clear strategic focus means that such investments may end up being a waste of resources. A successful organization will have a clearly articulated strategy that sets the direction for all its investments and activities. Such a strategy identifies and outlines the expected value to be achieved in terms that can be understood by its key stakeholders. These high-level strategic goals will serve as metrics that, when measured, will determine whether the goals have been achieved or not. It is in the strategy development process that the value outcomes are discussed, articulated, and solidified. For example, a corporation's goal may be to improve profitability through cost reduction. A service organization, public or private, might wish to address client response time. These types of goals serve as beacons for decisions made throughout the organization.

It is the responsibility of senior leaders to set the strategic direction. Administrative and operational staff do provide input into the strategy. This strategy must be communicated throughout, and beyond, the organization. To provide guidance for decisions and activities, everyone must hear and comprehend it. This helps to create common understanding as to what is expected.

Without a clear strategy, organizations may become directionless, lurching from one crisis to another, while making decisions that may ultimately increase the likelihood of not attaining value outcomes. The strategy is the rudder that will help the organization navigate the storms that are an inevitable part of organizational life. Even if the strategy has to change, which is often the case, change of direction and activities will be made from a well-defined and understood starting point. This will foster better and dynamic alignment of goals, activities, and metrics across the organization.

Investment

To achieve the strategy, the organization must decide what investments to make and where, when, and how those investments will be made. When it comes to IT, there are many options for making investments that could yield the same results. IT investments do not get priority over other types of investments simply because they are IT. IT investments must be able to compete with other types of investment to earn the money and other resources necessary. For that to happen, those proposing IT investments must be able to state the outcomes to be accomplished in business terms, consistent with the strategy. For example, if the goal is to increase profitability by reducing cost, then any IT project proposed must be able to communicate how it will reduce cost and what the ensuing impact on profitability will be. In that way, the IT investment can be compared to other competing investments such as new machinery or staff training. IT should have no special guarantee for its part of the investment fund.

Asset

Once an investment decision is made, processes and activities are enacted to ensure the design, acquisition, and deployment of the IT asset. The asset could be an entire application system, a website, a network, or anything that can be used to achieve a strategic goal. Prior to making investments in acquiring assets, leaders must also recognize that acquiring one asset may require significant investment in other complementary assets. Enabling online shopping, for example, may mean more investment in the technology infrastructure.

Putting the asset into production does not mean the strategic value sought has been achieved. The asset, after being put into production, must be used appropriately and adroitly for the purpose it was developed to create a business impact. Effective use of an IT asset is not guaranteed, as IT assets can be wholly misused or underused, intentionally or unintentionally. Even if properly used, the asset may not deliver the expected impact because factors in the environment might have changed. Leaders in organizations must constantly and consistently assess if asset use is contributing to value realization. If it is not, the decisions need to be taken right away to adjust activities to suit the new realities.

Impact

To generate a business impact, the asset is applied to the business for the purposes it was created. For business impact to occur, business processes may need to be further modified to ensure that the systems are performing as planned or better. Generating superior business impact is not automatic. It requires careful attention to people management and culture change. Business impacts are created by people acting mindfully and appropriately in support of organization goal attainment. They are not created simply because sophisticated technology has been deployed. In many instances, the changes generated by new asset deployment may lead to people's resisting and even counterimplementing the changes. IT implementation potentially brings huge political and social upheaval to the organization. The IT department should not be responsible for business impact delivery and appropriation. Business units are responsible for generating business impact. Business units have to own the processes related to impact generation. IT provides support to these efforts.

Outcome

The ultimate outcome envisaged by the investment decision can only be achieved if the business impact generated is appropriately harvested. Harvesting business impacts is often a difficult process because of the potential for other forces in the environment to divert the gains made. Appropriating the business value requires proficient, incisive, and decisive action on the part of organizational leaders and members. The new outcome should be better than the old outcome, and that is the business value created. That business value should be directly tied to the return expected from the investment and expressed in terms consistent with the organizational strategy. The timing of value appropriation is also very important. It is always important to deliver "quick wins" to drive momentum and provide energy for change. However, full value delivery is often not possible in the short term. Managers must therefore ensure that they don't lose sight of the long-term potential for value delivery in their haste to move on to newer agendas.

One key outcome that senior leaders must be aware of is that the results of asset deployment and impact can be appropriated away for purposes other than the planned outcome. For example, the deployment of a faster, more robust IT network could mean that more people will use the network to do more things than they were able to do before, thus rendering the network just as congested as it previously was. While there might be value in this beneficial new use, it may mean that the planned outcome will not be achieved. Senior leaders must carefully manage this situation to ensure that the use to which the investment is put supports the goals of the organization. If the asset is put to unintended good uses, then further investment might have to be made to generate the additional value envisioned. Unintended use detrimental to the organization needs to be shut down as quickly as possible.

The Agricultural Model and the VRC

The processes identified in the VRC provide a great complement for the Agricultural Model of IT value delivery discussed earlier. Figure 5.2 below describes the relationship between the ideas.

Strategy development involves much planning. Like the farmer in agriculture, business leaders must articulate a strategy and plan of action that will

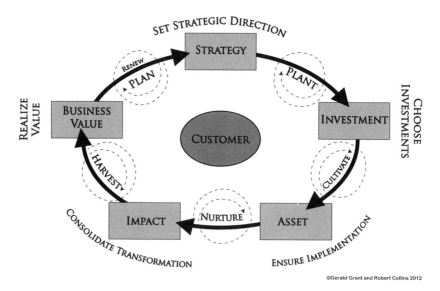

©Gerald Grant and Robert Collins 2012

Fig. 5.2 The agricultural model and the VRC

lead to the delivery of a rich harvest (business value). But planning alone is not sufficient. The plan must be enacted in practice.

The farmer, after deciding what harvest to target, must make an investment in identifying, acquiring, and planting the seed (or sapling) that will lead to the fully producing plant. Likewise in organizations. Organizational leaders must identify, acquire, and deploy the information technology that will create the asset that will provide the foundation for business value delivery. Once the investment is made and deployed, it must be cultivated.

A productive plant does not yield fruit (or seed grains) without careful cultivation by dedicated artisans. Similarly, IT asset creation results from careful cultivation by IT and business professionals. Robust and high-quality IT assets do not simply emerge out of a good design. Highly skilled professionals guided by effective project management are central to this process. Cultivation means ensuring that the plant (investment) survives and thrives. Many projects fail to make it to production. They have had to be abandoned. This is like having to abandon a field after it was planted. The investment, once lost, cannot be recovered.

Just because the asset is put into production doesn't mean that it will produce the results envisaged. It must be nurtured just like a plant that has survived the germination and cultivation processes. Nurturing involves activities that will ensure growth beyond the early survival stage toward the production and ripening of the fruit (grain) ready for harvest. IT assets must be successfully integrated into organizational life and functioning to produce the impacts desired.

These impacts are then carefully harvested to yield the business value planned for or obtainable in the circumstances.

By applying the ideas from the agricultural motif to the VRC, organizational leaders and members have a powerful set of ideas that can help them to navigate the dynamic and fraught process of generating value from IT investments. This does not provide a quick fix, which some leaders seek. It, however, realistically demonstrates how lasting value can be accomplished and what must be done to make this happen.

Applying the Agricultural Model to the VRC: Two Examples

Citizen-Centric Municipality

A municipal government wants to become more citizen-centric. It wishes to focus more directly on the experience of the citizens interacting with the municipality rather than focus on the internal workings of the municipal administration. Its goals in this include improved citizen satisfaction with the municipality and reduced cost for administration. To accomplish this **business value,** municipal executives would develop a **strategy** to be approved by the municipal council of elected representatives and communicated to the organization.

Investment to create self-service access to municipal services, allowing citizens to do things online instead of having them come to the town hall or deal with a live person over the phone, would be one way of meeting this **strategy.** The cost of the investment would be estimated along with the expected value to address both goals of citizen satisfaction (measured from a survey) and that of reduced cost (reduced effort by staff to perform functions that citizens can now do themselves online). The council would then approve this **investment** and fund it.

The service delivery department would then work with the IT department to develop (or acquire) an online self-serve system. For example, the bylaw department would work with IT to allow people to apply for a dog license over the Internet. The result of this **planting** would be a new online system for dog licenses.

That new system would then be tested and refined to make sure that it performed according to specifications and that there are no technical hitches (e.g., network performance) that would prevent the use of the new **asset.** This is the **cultivation** of the **asset.** The cultivation phase may uncover the need for a connection between the online system and the phone service, as users may have questions after they start online. Engaging in asset **cultivation** would ensure that the **asset** is ready to be deployed into production.

Upon launching the asset into production, the development team would stay with the project, training the users, listening to their feedback, and making adjustments to ensure that the expected value delivery is not jeopardized by unexpected technical, or nontechnical problems. This is the **nurturing** phase that ensures that the system will produce the business **impact** envisaged by the strategy.

The results of this process would then be **harvested.** In this example, that **harvest** should be a combination of reduced costs due to citizens doing the work themselves and increased satisfaction by citizens who can now access the service on a 7 × 24 basis.

This 7 × 24 service is the type of outcome that can easily prove problematic. In the past, the municipality only needed staff available from 9 to 5. No IT staff were required outside those hours. But now, it is possible for citizens to access this system any time of day. That is great for the people who no longer have to interrupt their busy day to go to the municipal office. But what if they should encounter technical problems? How can a citizen contact the municipality's IT department to get it fixed?

It may now be necessary to have IT staff on call throughout the day. This is going to increase costs—the exact opposite of the objective of reducing cost through less staff time. This is a good example of why you cannot stop after the planting and expect the harvest. If the municipality adds costs to support the new system, what is the impact on the harvest? It will be less. Perhaps it will be negative. A perfectly good asset will not create the value expected.

In Agricultural Model terms, this crop requires different cultivation and infrastructure than the previous crop. In a perfect world, this would have been discovered before the investment was made. However, such problems regularly arise in the real world. This is the improvisational management of change that the Agricultural Model embraces.

It is quite possible that, just for dog licensing, the returns do not justify the investment including the increased IT staff costs. But this is just one online system—one field on the farm. If a number of services were available online, the cost of the increased staffing in IT would be spread across the many systems rather than attached solely to dog licensing. The same person on call for the dog-licensing system could also support building permits, tax payments, swimming registration, and other systems. The IT staff costs are really infrastructure for the whole farm, supporting many fields. With this view of the whole farm, the investments return positive value where the focus on a single field (one system) would show a false negative result.

This knowledge, gained during the **cultivation** and **nurturing** phases of the project, can now be cycled back to the **strategy**. The municipality can review and **renew** its plan, adjust its investments with this knowledge in mind. That will affect future investments but keep the focus on the goals set by the council.

University Network

A university wanted to modernize its processes by putting courses and material online. The expected results are happier, more successful students and reduced costs from printing. That tied directly to a recruiting **strategy** for increasing enrollment.

To enable this, the university recognized that this would put a strain on the existing network. The IT department developed a plan to improve the network to meet these new needs. The university decided to **invest** in this new network. This is part of the **plan** to exploit technology more effectively.

The IT department procured equipment and services to create the new network. The result of this **planting** is a network that can handle ten times the traffic that the old network managed. This new **asset** is intended to support online access to material and even let students attend classes online or watch lectures on their own time.

During the **cultivation** of the new asset, the IT staff dealt with a number of problems including incompatible devices and network bottlenecks. Finally, they were prepared to put the new network into production to support the new processes.

Surprisingly, once in full use, the performance was far below expectations. IT was able to confirm that all the equipment was working correctly. Yet, the returns expected were not being achieved. The **harvest** was in jeopardy and **nurturing** was clearly required. IT monitored traffic and soon found the problem. Students, discovering the increased bandwidth available to them, had quickly exploited it, downloading videos and music, playing games, working on assignments, and staying in touch with friends. The value, expected in course and material delivery, had been appropriated by the students for other purposes that were valuable to them. This was the equivalent of pests invading the field and consuming the crop before it was harvested and sent to market.

Careful review identified that this unplanned harvest was not completely at odds with the university strategy. Happy students were making people aware on social media of how great things were at this university. That message was creating a positive impression that could be used in recruiting—a strategic goal. Eliminating this unexpected harvest would have the reverse effect. Careful, adroit management was necessary here to nurture this asset along the lines originally intended without undermining a key strategy.

Further **cultivation** and **nurturing** led to the university's being able to achieve the intended goals as well as reap some of the unexpected **harvest** the students had appropriated. **Cultivation** took the form of traffic shaping through policies on the network that discriminated at different times, prioritizing some traffic over others. The **nurturing** took the form of communicating with students, ensuring they weren't surprised by the traffic shaping and enlisting them to help manage demand by appealing to their need to access the courses and material now online.

Without the focus on the **harvest** and the resulting **cultivation** and **nurturing**, the project would have failed. A perfectly good **asset** would have resulted from the **planting** but the value, appropriated by the students, would not have achieved the **strategic** goal. A knee-jerk reaction to the problem, such as prohibiting students from downloading large files, could even have resulted in a negative impact to that strategy.

Time and the VRC

Once of the most important contributions of a process-based framework such as the VRC is the understanding that value delivery takes place over time. Time matters. There is what we call a temporal dynamic to business value delivery from IT investment. Every investment goes through temporal stages of development. The whole VRC can take a lot of time—usually years. The extent and speed of the VRC process across the temporal boundaries depend to a large extent on the type of investment being made and the context in which that investment is being made.

We suggest five stages of development for IT investment to yield business value. They are initiation, inscription, diffusion, legitimation, and stabilization. These are depicted in Fig. 5.3.

Initiation relates to the idea generation and planning stages of the VRC. It is in this stage that the business ideas are developed and the business case is made. The development of a strategy for an organization usually takes the better part of a year. Many stakeholders must be engaged. Many options need to be considered. Reducing a large number of good ideas to a focused, workable number is a difficult task. Once this is done, there must be a proactive process of communication that ensures that the strategy is understood by everyone in the organization, and often outside it.

The process of developing, assessing, prioritizing, and deciding upon investments requires intensive and comprehensive communication across the organization. There are hard decisions to make. Most often, there are many more good investment ideas than there is time, money, or resources to carry them out. Careful decision making is needed. Again, this must be followed by clear communication so that everyone understands what is being undertaken and what results are expected. Applying appropriate methods (agile, joint application design (JAD), prototyping, and others), business and IT personnel engage in translating the plan into action. This can take from six months to a year to complete. This is the inscription phase.

The asset, once created, is made available to users through a process that involves training (in-class, computer-based training (CBT), hands-on) and experimental use. This is the diffusion phase. The goal here is to get as many people familiar with the asset as possible. Once people become familiar with the IT asset, they may begin to use it in doing their jobs. This time can vary depending upon the asset being created. For some IT projects, such as an ERP implementation, three years to achieve the first harvest is not out of the question.

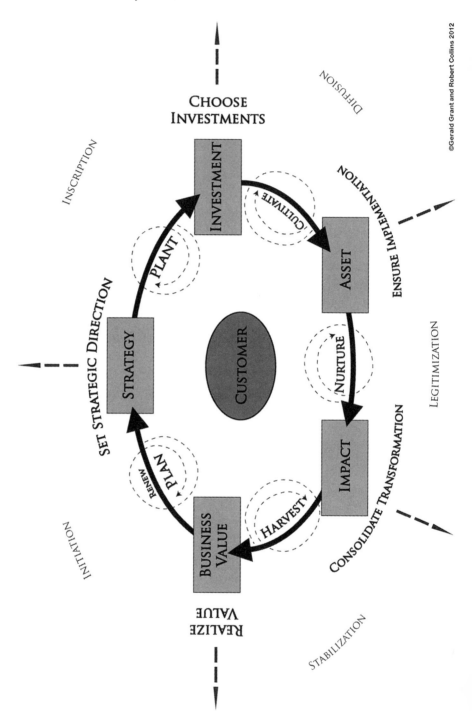

Fig. 5.3 The temporal aspects of the VRC

The extent to which use is voluntary or required will determine how well and how quickly the use becomes legitimized in the organization. The more the use of the IT asset becomes the accepted way of doing things in the organization, the more legitimized it becomes. The Agricultural Model describes the nurturing period during which the business processes are honed to maximize the resulting harvest. The success of nurturing will affect the adoption and effectiveness of the new technology and processes. The legitimation phase is crucial to success because if the use of the asset lacks legitimacy, it will not become engrained in the organization's routines and processes. For example, if organizational leaders allow the old processes to continue (e.g., the use of paper and pen), then it will be difficult to legitimate the new approach.

Stabilization is the final phase. Here the new system and processes have become the accepted way for the organization to function now and into the future. The harvest, the realization of value from the investment, occurs in this phase. This harvesting of value occurs regularly, usually measured annually. It is when this harvesting has occurred that effective measurement of outcomes can be done. It can take several years for the harvest to achieve the return predicted in the original investment plan. The stabilization phase can go on for years. Large IT investments can rarely deliver results in less than three years and often take four to five years. However, leaders must be vigilant to ensure that they are not lulled into thinking that all is well. The amount of external change that can happen over such a period, as well as the lessons learned during regular internal review and renewal, emphasize the need for a good "weather eye" and strong change management skills that are the bedrock of the Agricultural Model.

Governance Processes and Mechanisms and the VRC

In putting forward the VRC, the question is often asked, What about the well-known processes and mechanisms for managing IT that are widely used in practice by organizations? How do these relate to the VRC? Are they replaced by something else? The short answer is that the VRC does not replace these well-established methods. It redefines when and how these methods are used and what value they bring to ensuring business value realization.

Figure 5.4 outlines some of the most common mechanisms that are applied in governing and managing investments in IT.

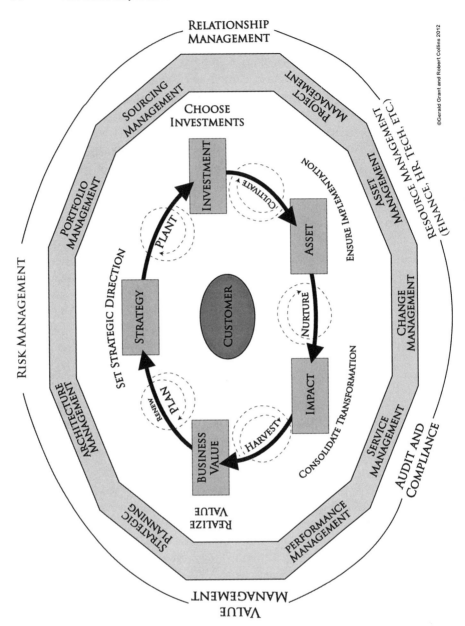

Fig. 5.4 Governance processes and the VRC

One of the biggest problems with the processes and mechanisms as they are currently applied in practice is that they are often viewed as ends in themselves. Some organizations place an inordinate amount of value on project management, for instance. Often, delivery of the IT project on budget, within scope, and on time becomes the sole preoccupation of the project team. When the project is deployed, the project team celebrates and moves on, often oblivious of what will happen afterward. By applying the VRC, we demonstrate that there is a lot more to be done to realize value from investments. The deployment of a completed IT project just takes us to the asset creation phase. The asset must be nurtured, instituting complementary change, and asset and service management. Business value realization is supported by performance management and value management processes and mechanisms. All of these are additionally supported by adroit resource and risk management. Through audit and compliance processes, organizations ensure that they meet required legal, regulatory, and quality standards.

In Summary

The VRC presents a comprehensive way of framing discussion and understanding of how organizations can realize, in practice, business value from IT investments. It treats the value realization process as an integrated series of processes and activities that are necessary, but at the same time insufficient on their own, to deliver the value sought. Interwoven with each of the processes is the element of time. This illustrates, not only that there is a series of activities that must be accomplished, but that these activities have temporal aspects that make it impossible to draw a direct link between the investment in and creation of an IT asset and ultimate realized business value.

How value is realized can be understood in terms associated with the agricultural cycle, planning, planting, cultivating, nurturing, harvesting, and renewing. The agricultural approach allows organizations to be both structured and flexible since in agriculture there are many unknowns that must be managed along the way. By keeping a "weather eye," leaders and members in organizations can anticipate and innovatively respond to unexpected change.

The VRC embraces the application of well-known and well-used IT management processes and mechanisms. It, however, shapes the way they are used, and reinterprets the value they may contribute to the overall goal of delivering business value outcomes.

Discussion Questions

1. Identify a recent IT project that you have been involved with. Discuss how applying the VRC ideas may have influenced how the project was designed, executed, and measured in your organization.
2. Explain whether and how the application of the Agricultural Model would alter your interpretation of what happened during project development, deployment, and operation.
3. What is your perspective on the role of time and related temporal dimensions in understanding when and how value might be delivered from investments in IT? How would this change how and when value is measured?
4. How would you justify the use of the VRC in the face of opposition to altering the prime role played by tried and true methods and mechanisms such as portfolio management and project management?

6

Governing IT Service Delivery

The first section of this book focused on new models that explain the value that is sought from information technology (IT) investments (the Value Cycle), the complex nature of IT investments intended to bring about change (the Agricultural Model), and the means whereby IT's efforts to create assets are translated into the desired goals of the organization (the Value Realization Cycle, or VRC). With these models in mind, the next few chapters will explore considerations that any organization must address—governance, communication, and sourcing.

In this chapter, we will focus on what we believe is the most important of these considerations—governance. If an organization gets governance right, then it has the means to deal with any problems that arise, regardless of how well it is making investments. If it does not have effective governance, there is a severely diminished likelihood that investments will produce value even when everything else is done well.

Most prominently reported failures in IT are largely failures in institutional and IT governance. While it is popular to blame technology, project managers, or service providers for IT failures, it is quite clear that many of these failures come back to decisions made or not made by those responsible for governing organizations. IT governance has gained prominence in recent years because of the renewed focus on corporate and institutional governance following the many financial and ethical scandals of the early 2000s. IT governance itself became more prominent because for many, it was the weak link in the governance chain. Not much attention had been given to IT governance by executives prior to that. However, new legal requirements regarding infor-

© The Editor(s) (if applicable) and The Author(s) 2016
G.G. Grant, R. Collins, *The Value Imperative*,
DOI 10.1057/978-1-137-59040-4_6

mation management, coupled with the fact that IT is consuming such a large proportion of organizational investments, have driven organizations to give more attention to the governance and management of IT.

IT governance determines who has authority for significant IT decisions and which executives are accountable and responsible for which IT activities at which level of the enterprise. Governance arrangements are usually manifested in structures, processes, and service delivery mechanisms. IT governance is a dynamic, performance-driven, adaptive, and relational process that focuses on synchronizing corporate and IT strategies, objectives, accountability structures, systems, and practices. Its core objective is to deliver valuable, risk-reduced, and measureable returns on IT-related investments.

IT governance should be distinguished from IT management. Management is about ensuring that the processes for achieving organizational objectives are executed according to the most efficient and effective methods. Once an objective is agreed upon, managers set about to plan and orchestrate how that objective will be reached. Management has accountabilities at all levels of the organization. Governance is about setting direction and objectives and ensuring that those who are accountable for program execution actually do their jobs. It is also about setting standards of performance and ensuring that mechanisms are put in place by which accomplishments can be monitored, measured, and evaluated. Governance also occurs at all levels of the organization.

All too often, governance meetings proceed as follows: Senior management is assembled to get an update on the project. The IT project manager runs the meeting and elaborates on a great many things that have happened. During this time, the senior management check their email and think about something else. Then the project manager indicates that the project is going to be two months late. Senior managers express their dissatisfaction and ask why, seeking who to blame. The various department representatives defend their areas and cast blame elsewhere. Senior managers then start asking about various details seeking to find a way to put the project back on schedule. This does not work, as they lack the understanding of the minutiae necessary to make the correct decisions. An agreement is made to cut the delay by one month by dropping some functionality and cutting training. No one assesses the impact that these changes will have on the business value that was to be achieved. Everyone leaves unhappy. In two months, the exercise is repeated.

What would good governance look like? Looking back to our previous example, when everyone arrived at the governance meeting, they would have already known about the delay. This would have been discussed by the project team who would have assessed the various options to address the situation.

Senior management would have been provided with a list of these options with the focus on the impact to business value (harvest) and changes to the originally approved return on investment (ROI). The discussion at this meeting would remain at the level of the harvest with the senior managers' making a decision as to which option to choose. They would then direct the project team to adjust the project accordingly and update them at the next meeting.

Good IT governance builds trust among organizational stakeholders because it increases transparency in IT-related decision making. It also facilitates better delivery of IT projects because they will more likely be focused on supporting business goals. This will help in synchronizing business and IT strategies, ensuring that everyone is going in the same direction. Good IT governance promotes effective communication among stakeholders and encourages organizational members to work collaboratively, responsibly, and effectively.

Dimensions of IT Governance

Often, most discussion of IT governance revolves around structural elements: configuration (centralized, decentralized, federal), levels (board through operating), accountability (who is responsible for what outcomes), and rights (decision, input, consultative). These are all important aspects of governance. However, governance also has other dimensions that will shape how it is configured and executed in practice. These include the nature of sourcing relationships, the processes that are enacted, the temporal characteristics that define the organization, and the general environmental context that shapes organizational activities. Figure 6.1 outlines the key dimensions and elements of governance that need to be considered when considering governance of IT service delivery in organizations.

The structural dimension of IT governance is prominent in much of the writings on governance. Peter Weill and Jeanne Ross[1] use the term "archetypes" to identify the various configurations IT governance structures may take. The archetypes they suggest include Business Monarchy, IT Monarchy, Feudal, federal, IT Duopoly, and Anarchy. Each of these configurations denotes who makes decisions about IT. For example, in a business monarchy, configuration decisions about IT are made by an executive committee, an operating committee, an investment council, or the CEO. In contrast, in an IT monarchy, deci-

---

[1] Weill, P. and Ross, J. W. (2004) IT Governance: How top performers manage IT decisions rights for superior results, Boston, Harvard Business Press.

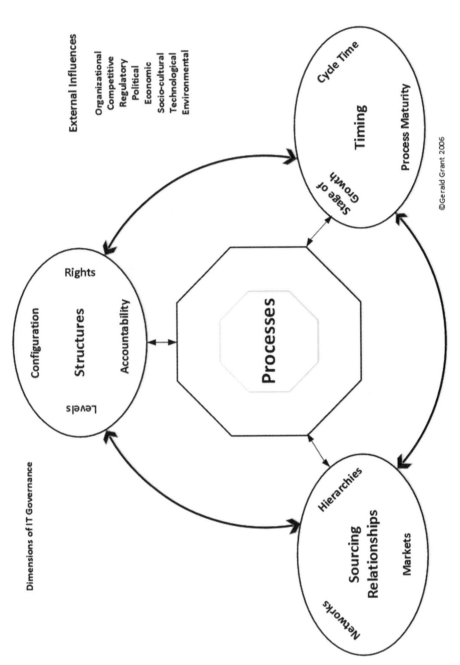

Fig. 6.1   Dimensions of IT governance

sions about IT are made by an IT leadership council, an IT executive, or the chief information officer (CIO). Anarchy represents the situation where each individual user makes IT decisions for himself or herself without reference to an organizational plan. Weill and Ross's archetypes extend the often-cited centralized, decentralized, and federal configurations for IT governance structures.

Accountability structures represent another aspect of the structural dimensions of governance. Who is accountable for what and to what extent is important if governance is to be effective. If there is no accountability, then governance will be ineffective or even fall apart. Effective governance means that organizational executives must identify and allocate the various accountabilities and responsibilities for all individuals and groups within the governance structures. Accountabilities and responsibilities are typically allocated according to hierarchical levels in the organizations. Figure 6.2 provides a generic representation of a typical IT governance arrangement. The board of directors is typically accountable for setting policy direction and mandates, allocating resources, and monitoring and evaluating performance and compliance with stated goals and objectives. One area that has galvanized board attention in recent years is around IT security and privacy. Significant security breaches at Sony, Target, and Home Depot, to name a few, have resulted in billions of dollars in losses to companies. Boards have reacted to these events by firing CEOs and CIOs. In some of these cases, however, it is clear that the boards themselves may have been less vigilant than they should have been.

Corporate executives and their executive steering committees are responsible for setting and articulating corporate business and IT strategies, establishing priorities for IT investment and resource allocation, and ensuring that the organization achieves its strategic objectives. Setting priorities is a key aspect of IT governance that can only be effectively done by corporate executives working together. Often this is an area of weakness in organizations. Many times, priority setting is neglected and what is done amounts to rubberstamping decisions already made informally or accepting what has already been done as *fait accompli*. Priority setting amounts to simply horse trading of projects among business managers.

The corporate IT management group is responsible for establishing and enforcing enterprise architecture policies and standards. This group is primarily responsible for articulating IT strategy in coordination with the overall corporate business strategy. On the supply side, they must plan, source, deliver, and manage enterprise-wide IT systems and services in response to organizational requirements. Business unit IT groups are responsible for articulating business-specific IT needs and working cooperatively with IT and other business units to ensure the service required is delivered.

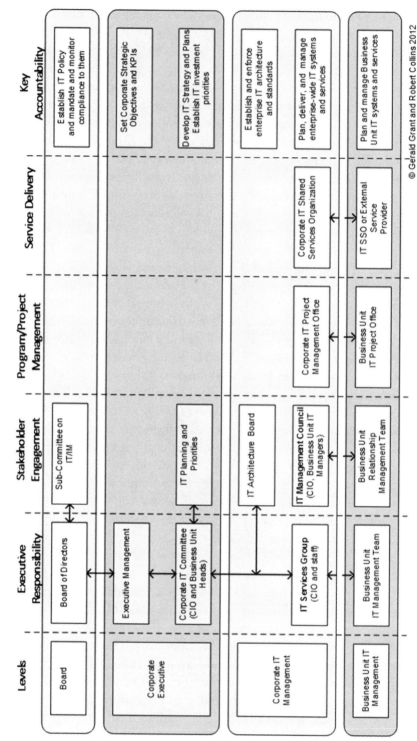

Generic IT Governance Structure

© Gerald Grant and Robert Collins 2012

Within the governance structure, different parties have the right to make decisions, to be consulted, to provide input, and to be informed of decisions and actions taken. Understanding who is accountable for making each type of IT decision is essential for transparency and clarity. For example, in an organization where IT governance is structured as a business monarchy, deciding on IT investment priorities is the responsibility of the corporate IT steering committee, not the CIO acting alone. Within the IT service delivery organization, the CIO is in charge and is accountable for all decisions made within the IT unit. If decision-making structures are unclear, the potential for conflict increases and creates delays. Such conflict may make it difficult to institute effective governance mechanisms. Although some stakeholder groups may not have decision rights, they may have the right to be consulted for their input into decisions, especially if the decision will affect them personally or their area of work. Business unit managers and staff need to be consulted when decisions taken elsewhere will affect them, whether positively or negatively. Taking decisions without the appropriate consultation with other stakeholders is a recipe for disaster. Other stakeholders may have the right to be informed of decisions taken. Although not involved in the decision-making process, these persons may need to be informed of the decision taken, especially if it will have a negative impact. Keeping stakeholders informed increases the opportunity for enhancing communication among them. Recognition and respect for the rights of each stakeholder group is fundamental to good governance. Without this, any governance arrangement will become ineffective.

IT Service-Sourcing Relationships

Organizations have options for provisioning IT services that will shape how governance is carried out in practice. Services can be provisioned internally through the organizational hierarchy. This means that the organization itself will invest in developing an internal IT services group that will design, develop, and deploy IT services. For some organizations, this is the appropriate choice. Other organizations will look to the market to provision IT services. Typically called outsourcing, some organizations believe that they can get the best results from contracting out the service provisioning because of the wide availability of reliable and trustworthy providers. By outsourcing this part of their business, they can then focus on their core business competencies. By going to the market they can offload the cost and complexity of keeping pace with an increasingly complex technological environment. By buying in services, they leave the burden of keeping up-to-date with the service provider. A third way of provisioning services is through peer networks. Here, rather than the hierarchy of the internal IT group or the buyer-seller relationship of markets, several peer organizations work together jointly to deliver common IT services. Typically, these shared services arrangements seek to take the best of both the hierarchy and the market to deliver services that on one hand are cost-effective while at the same time highly focused on the business and what it seeks to achieve.

Governing in a hierarchy is very different from governing in a market arrangement. Network governance differs as well from both hierarchy and markets. In a hierarchy, governance revolves around the exercise of administrative power. Managers in the hierarchy have the authority to command and control the behavior of organizational units. They can make or alter decisions based on their understanding of organizational priorities. Hierarchies are most efficient and effective when obtaining services in the market carry high transaction costs. If markets are not well-developed, then organizations are better off doing things themselves. In many circumstances, however, the IT services required are easily obtained in the market.

Currently, there are many organizations providing cloud-based infrastructural and applications services. For example, organizations can easily get software applications such as email, word processing, enterprise resource planning (ERP), customer relationship management (CRM), sales force automation, and other application services provisioned by software as a service (SaaS) organizations such as Google, Microsoft, Oracle, Salesforce.com, and many others. Platform and infrastructural services (PaaS and IaaS) can be bought from Amazon, Rackspace, Microsoft, and other providers. All this makes it easy for organizations to get up and running quickly without having to invest in their own IT department. They simply buy the services they need. In a market situation, the key to governing is contract management and service agreements. Much focus must be put on selecting the right supplier, ensuring that the contract signed is right for the organization, and making sure that the supplier delivers the services contracted for on the basis of the service agreements entered into. The leverage the organization has is that it can switch service providers if the one originally contracted fails to deliver satisfactorily. Switching is easier said than done, however. Often, services become embedded with those of the service provider, making it difficult to switch even if desired.

When services are being provisioned jointly in a network, the ability to command action, as typically found in a hierarchy, or the threat posed by the ability to switch providers in a market, are significantly diminished. Networks are joint activity engaged in voluntarily. Consequently, there are no superior-subordinate or buyer-seller relationships. Networks come about because organizations want to engage in joint activity to benefit the group. Governing in networks then is most effectively done through building trusting relationships with network members. Each member must see and receive value from the joint activity. Networks will fall apart if only one party benefits. Networks are difficult to set up and manage. However, they have great potential for delivering on the best aspects of hierarchical and market arrangements. That is why many corporations, governments, and not-for-profit organizations have looked to shared services arrangements to deliver IT and other transactional services.

Nowadays, there are almost no scenarios where service provisioning is purely hierarchical, market based, or networked. Service delivery typically involves a mix of these modes. Therefore, governing IT becomes more complicated and nuanced. What is important to understand is that governance of IT is not a one-size-fits-all situation. The types of IT service delivery arrangements will affect how governance is approached and enacted in practice. Managers need to be aware of this and ensure that they have the capacity and processes in place to deal with the different arrangements. If most services will be delivered through market-based mechanisms, the organization needs to ensure it has significant capacity in contract and service management. In network-based delivery scenarios, relationship management along with training for key players becomes a significant capability need.

The Temporal Dimensions of IT Governance

Time plays an important role in governance. The temporal aspects of governance are manifested in issues related to where the organization is in its stage of growth, the maturity of its governance processes, and the cycle time for executing its business model. An organization goes through general stages of growth from birth, growth, maturity, decline, renewal, or death. At each stage of the organizational development cycle, different combinations of IT governance practices become prominent. At birth, much focus is on survival and "crossing the chasm".[2] Here very little emphasis it put on formal IT governance. As organizations begin to grow, most effort is put on setting direction, setting priorities, and allocating resources. In the mature stage of growth, there is significant focus on service management, control and compliance, and performance management. As organizations face decline, even more emphasis tends to be put on control. If the organization is to renew itself, a lot more focus should be put on setting a new direction. To effectively govern the

---

[2] Moore, G. (2005) Dealing with Darwin: How great companies innovate in every phase of their evolution, New York, Penguin.

IT organization, executives must be aware of where the organization is in its development cycle. With this awareness, they can then select the mechanisms that will best fit the requirements of that stage of development.

Organizations with very mature governance processes are better able to handle the complexities of a diverse and ever-evolving IT investment environment. Governance maturity levels can be classified as incomplete, performed, managed, established, predictable, and optimized.[3] As with any maturity model, operating at the lowest levels of maturity is often problematic for organizations unless this is a deliberate strategic choice. It is often more costly to move from one stage of maturity to the other the higher up in the maturity stage one gets. Achieving the highest level of maturity, while desirable, may not be worth it from an incremental cost perspective. Most organizations are content operating between level 3 and level 5 of the maturity pyramid. Very few would seek to be fully optimized.

The cycle time between when investments are made and returns are expected may be either short or long depending on the organization and the industry sector in which it operates. A firm operating in a high-technology software or hardware industry might have a very short cycle time to show returns as compared with an organization in the mining industry. Government organizations face cycle times related to the election cycle for politicians. The retail industry pays much attention to seasonal variations. It is at these times that major decisions are made about what investments to pursue and what to prioritize. IT governance processes are shaped by these considerations of the business cycle. Managers need to know what the prevailing cycle time is for their organization and must manage accordingly. For example, technology investments that will take several years to deliver value may be a hard sell for a fast-moving technology organization. Such projects may need to be broken up into manageable chunks that more readily fit the business cycle of the company.

IT Governance Processes

What do executives do when they govern IT in organizations? This is a crucial question since governance goes beyond the structural, relational, and temporal dimensions. Many equate governance with having the right structures in place. However, having executive steering committees, IT investment boards, architecture and standards councils, and other structural elements are not suf-

---

[3] ISACA, (2011) COBIT 5: The framework, Exposure Draft. p. 46.

ficient to guarantee good IT governance. Governance must be enacted in practice on a daily basis. There must not only be a façade of governance, it must happen, in reality. Governance in practice is manifested in the processes and mechanisms that are established and executed by managers on an ongoing basis.

A Delphi survey of practicing CIOs[4] identified a number of IT governance processes that are crucial for effectively governing IT investments in organizations. These processes are depicted in Fig. 6.3. As discussed earlier, for organizations to realize value from IT investments, they must set a strategic direction for IT, choose the IT investments that they will make, ensure that the investments made are implemented, consolidate the required organizational transformation, and ensure value is harvested in an effective and appropriate manner.

The model in Fig. 6.3 depicts five overarching governance processes that are the key accountability of executive management and the board of directors. These are risk management, relationship management, resource management, audit and compliance, and value management. These five processes encompass what must be done at the highest levels to ensure investment success.

Risk management is a key accountability of the CEO of an organization and the board of directors. In managing risks, organizational executives must ensure that the appropriate IT investment is being made and that all IT projects are prioritized based on success factors and expected return. Business and IT risks need to be identified, evaluated, and effectively managed. Organizational board members and executives must understand the risk profile and stance for their organizations. Without significant risk management acuity, executives can "bet" the company. Recent Examples, such as the security breach at Ashley Madison demonstrate how seemingly inconsequential decisions can lead to large-scale failures, significant financial losses, and loss of credibility.

Governance is, at its heart, an intensely relational process. While it is relatively easy to have a governance framework on paper, it is much more difficult to enact it in practice. Governance is enacted in relationships between stakeholders. Whether enacted in hierarchies, markets, or networks, it is the mutually beneficial relationships that drive achievement of organizational objectives. Key to effective ***relationship management*** is understanding who the stakeholders are and what is important in driving their engagement with the strategic goals and objectives of the organization. In managing relationships, stakeholder concerns need to be understood and taken into account. While all concerns cannot be fully addressed at any one time, it must be clear

---

[4] Grant, G. This is from ongoing current research on IT governance processes.

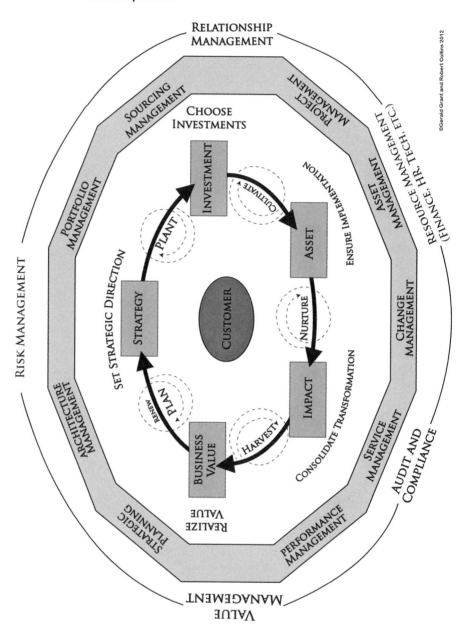

Fig. 6.3.   IT governance processes and the VRC

to stakeholders why certain decisions were made and others not. This will build trust in the governance process, which is its lifeblood. Without trust, governance can end up being an endless stream of debilitating power games. Such power dynamics, if left unchecked, can make it difficult for organizations to find consensus on value. As a result, organizations may end up making costly and unnecessary investments that may even undermine their strategic intent.

Any governance structure or process will fail in practice if there isn't effective and sufficient *resource management*. Resources (including finance, talent, technology, space, and others) are the fuel of governance execution in practice. Without adequate financial resources, governance options are constrained and often impossible to implement. All options have resource implications. If there is no money, people, technology, or space, it is highly unlikely that the organization will accomplish what it has set out to do. Even if there are adequate resources, simply allocating them without consideration of strategic priorities and ROI will lead to substantial waste. Resources have to be judiciously managed to deliver the value sought by the organization. Demand for resources puts enormous pressure on organizational executives. Powerful coalitions are likely to demand and get more resources than weaker ones. It is crucial that in allocating resources, steps are taken to ensure that investments in foundational and fundamental projects are given some priority. For example, it is always easier to get buy-in for investing in some new exciting technology. It is much harder to get resources allocated to operational IT infrastructure. Not investing in the operational infrastructure can lead to colossal failure in ongoing operations. Expecting great innovation on a weak and faulty platform is like setting off on an epic journey in a leaky boat. CIOs are accountable for ensuring the integrity of the operational IT infrastructure. They must ensure, through effective planning and articulation, that the required investments are made when needed.

A primary accountability in any governance framework is to ensure *control and compliance* with established legal, regulatory, and policy requirements. Organizations must audit their activities to ensure they are focused on achieving the strategic objectives of the organizations while complying with legal, regulatory, and policy directives and imperatives. Organizations need to have in place processes for managing legal and regulatory requirements. It cannot be left to chance. They must have the appropriate audit and compliance mechanisms in place to ensure that things are on the right track in terms of expected costs and benefits, and that, if not, corrections can be made in a timely fashion. Compliance accountabilities are distributed among executives with the CEO having the ultimate responsibility. For example, under

Sarbanes-Oxley[5], both the CEO and CFO (chief financial officer) must guarantee the integrity of the financial statements for publicly traded companies.

Value management focuses on ensuring that the value sought is delivered and harvested as projected. It is an ongoing process that focuses on ensuring that the value generated by IT investments is appropriated by the organization where it is most beneficial. Value can easily be misappropriated and applied to nonstrategic endeavors. For example, investments in renewing IT infrastructure can lose their intended effect if that new infrastructure is allowed to be applied to nonessential activities (for example, downloading music and movies for personal use). Executives need to focus on ensuring that IT investments provide the tangible advantages sought by the organization. This includes setting the parameters to measure returns on investment, both quantitatively and qualitatively.

The model in Fig. 6.3 highlights additional IT governance process elements that are an essential part of governing IT investments in organizations. Each of these elements generates questions that should be asked by practicing managers as they seek to govern IT-related activity. The governance process elements and questions are depicted in Table 6.1.

Governance in Practice—How to Use It

Governance must be instituted and supported by the highest levels of management. Indeed, it must start at that level. This is vital for two reasons. First, it is through this high-level governance that IT is tied to organizational strategy. Second, it is from this mandate that all levels of governance gain their legitimacy. Having set up a governance structure, executive management must make use of it as the primary communication and decision-making vehicle. Bypassing the governance arrangement undermines its role and will eventually cause it to fail. That will lead to a reduction in the value achieved from IT.

Governance bodies must have clearly defined roles, membership, and terms of reference. It must be clear who is meeting, how often, to do what, and what is expected from each governance body. It must be clear who reports to which governance body and to whom each governance body reports. The terms of reference should provide focus and should not seek to be all-encompassing. For example, the terms of reference for a senior governance body should be focused on value to be achieved and on the entire enterprise. They should

---

[5] Sarbanes Oxley Act of 2002 Corporate Responsibility, Public Law 107-204-July 30, 2002 (107th Congress), accessed April 29, 2016 https://www.sec.gov/about/laws/soa2002.pdf.

Table 6.1. Key governance questions

Process element	Key governance questions	Who is accountable?
Strategic planning	• Does IT properly support corporate strategy? • Do IT objectives and goals align with corporate objectives and goals? • Is IT an enabling presence in the organization?	Board CEO, CFO, CIO Business Line Executives
Architecture definition	• Are business and IT architecture principles developed and communicated? • Are architecture standards developed and enforced?	CEO, CFO, CIO Business Line Executives
Portfolio selection	• Is a portfolio approach applied when making IT investments? • Is the portfolio appropriately weighted to support ongoing operations as well as innovation and growth • Is the portfolio managed according to the risk profile of the organization?	CEO, CFO, CIO Business Line Executives
Sourcing	• Are sourcing principles and strategies articulated and communicated? • Are sourcing options appropriately identified and evaluated? • Are sourcing arrangements in line with the risk/reward profile of the organization?	CFO, CIO Business Line Executives
Project oversight	• Are project plans realistic and achievable? • Are projects appropriately structured and resourced? • Was the planned asset delivered?	CIO PMO Business Line Executives
Asset Stewardship	• Is there a full inventory of assets in the portfolio? • Are assets up-to-date and functioning? • Is there a plan to refresh and renew assets?	CFO, CIO Business Line Executives
Change management	• Is there a transformation plan? • Are change management processes in place?	Business Line Executives CIO PMO
Service management	• Are processes in place to ensure service delivery and continuity? • Are services functioning reliably and securely?	CIO IT Operations
Performance management	• Are performance objectives identified, articulated, and communicated? • Have appropriate measures been developed and applied? • Is performance measured and reported?	Board CEO, CFO, CIO Business Line Executives

indicate that specific projects will be overseen by lower-level governance bodies. Equally, the focus should be limited to governance matters and not cross into the realm of management. Higher-level governance bodies (such as the executive steering committee) can hold managers accountable for broad objectives but should not seek to tell them how to do their jobs.

Membership of governance bodies must be consistent with their function. At a senior level, the entire organization must be effectively represented. This does not necessarily mean that there must be one person there from every department. It does mean that any department can have a voice when it needs it, has someone to look out for their requirements and responsibilities, and can get effective and timely communication.

Well-run meetings are the cornerstone of effective governance. This may seem like motherhood, but meetings that are improperly structured and run are a common problem that causes governance to fail. Meetings for the sake of meeting produce disinterest and lack of involvement. That, in turn, undermines the effectiveness of governance and will eventually lead to failure. Well-run meetings with a clear agenda, well-written minutes communicating clear decisions and action items, distributed widely and in a timely fashion are essential for good governance.

Communication is key. Many people focus solely on governance bodies as decision makers. This, of course, is a primary role. But a decision that is not communicated is as ineffective as a decision not made. Effective communication includes not only the decisions but also the rationale for those decisions. If those rationales are properly guided by organizational objectives, they become uniting factors that create alignment throughout the organization. If they are not driven by organizational objectives, or not communicated effectively, then they become subjects of discussion and dissent that undermine alignment.

Governance is guided by, and provides guidance by, measures. A clearly defined harvest, expressed as ROI, and measurable organizational objectives are the province of governance. Initially, it is the role of governance bodies to communicate these measures. In making investment decisions, it is these measures that guide governance. In communicating decisions, the measures that will be used to assess results must be the cornerstone. Then, in meetings, evaluating against the previously defined and communicated measures is the very essence of governance's oversight role.

Governance is often seen as a limiting factor, taking away from people's ability to innovate and affect their environment. If this is the case, then it is a sign of bad governance. Done well, governance provides a means for anyone to influence the organization. It provides a destination for ideas. It provides a means and a formula to express opportunities in ways that tie them to organizational strategy. It ensures involvement of all the affected departments in the key decisions and keeps lines of communications open. When done well, governance creates enthusiasm and provides a means to have a say when it most matters.

Governance—What If?

Politics and Governance

No matter what structures are put in place, some people will seek to work around them when they cannot get what they want through normal channels. We often refer to this as "politics". In any organization, this is going to happen. Does this not fatally undermine governance? No. In fact, it makes governance even more important. Without a clear plan and a means to legitimize that plan for the organization, the politics of personal influence is the only way to get things done. In such an anarchic environment, it is virtually impossible to determine if the right priority is rising to the top. Equally, it is impossible to know that any project will stay on top. Whatever one person can shift one day, another can shift the next day.

With a proper governance structure, the impact of a sudden or arbitrary change can be made crystal clear. It can be shown that it is not a problem for IT, but rather for the groups whose previously approved work is being sidelined by this sudden change. The governance structure also provides a vehicle to communicate these issues. At the least, it can work to minimize the damage of an arbitrary override of the approved process and plan.

When such an arbitrary override occurs, it is important not only to assess the impact on the plan but to understand why the process was not able to handle the situation. Were the organizational goals unclear? Was there a lack of participation in the process? Was there a change in circumstances that warranted re-evaluation (the weather eye)? Was there a lack of commitment from some? The CIO's role here should be to find the flaw in the process and address it. It should not be to act as the police to enforce the decisions of the governance bodies. That is the role of those bodies themselves. The CIO should make these bodies aware of the specific issue(s) and ask them to address the situation. Then, drawing on relationships with other stakeholders, the CIO should seek to address the issues in the governance.

Governance regimes will always have to deal with exceptions. When this occurs, it is important to remember how much easier it is to deal with these exceptions when there is a governance process and how much worse it would be if there were no governance at all. Do not let these exceptions destroy the overwhelming benefits of good governance.

How Can You Manage a Lack of Participation?

It is common, when governance is first implemented, to find that some portion of the organization does not participate. They may pay lip service to governance, but it will be clear that they are not committing to making it work. How do you handle this situation?

A common mistake is to use governance to ostracize these "rebels": "If they won't participate, then none of their projects will get done". This is neither realistic nor helpful. It will merely push the nonparticipating groups to rebel against the process and try to destroy it. It is more important to try to understand why a group is not participating and address those specific issues. It may be a lack of understanding, a lack of skills in that department, poor management, or another cause. It is necessary to address the root causes; that is the only sure way to bring a recalcitrant group on board. Such an effort often needs to draw on the various levels of governance as well as the leadership skills of the CIO and his or her office.

Another common mistake is for IT and the CIO to be the enforcers of the rules. This actually goes against the purpose of governance. Organization governance is there to make organizational decisions and give organizational direction to IT. The plan it produces and oversees is not IT's plan, it is the organization's plan. Therefore, the organization as a whole, either through the governance bodies or the management structure, must be the one to enforce the governance rules. IT can support this but should not be the police force.

These two ideas can be combined very effectively. While the governance and/or management structure is challenging a group that is not participating, IT can be supportive. Instead of piling on with the enforcement effort, IT can approach the group in question and offer help to bridge the gap between them and the governance process. This puts IT on the good side of everyone and fulfills its role as a service organization.

Getting Executive Support for Governance

Regardless of how the issue is approached, it is vital that it be backed by executive management. If executives reward, or ignore, a lack of participation, then they are undermining governance. This leaves only peer pressure as a means to bring departments on side. In this case, the CIO must work to convince executive management to actively support the governance arrangements instituted by showing their benefits and articulating the damage that a lack of effective governance can do. Quite often, the best means of doing this is to produce the business case for governance. Make it clear what is at stake if governance is not successful and what can be achieved if it is. Then track that business case as you move forward to reinforce the idea that governance is not bureaucracy, it is a vital tool to a successful organization and the attainment of organizational goals.

Governance Example—Metro City

Metro City is a midsized municipality of one million people. It provides services to these people including transit, roads, water, sewers, parks and recreation, social services, fire, ambulance, bylaw services, planning, library, and public health services. The total budget for these services is in the neighborhood of $3 billion dollars. Like other governments in the second decade of the twenty-first century, the municipality was facing a squeeze with demands for more services but restraints on revenues and funding.

The chief operating officer (COO) of the city understood that IT was key to meeting these challenges. Three years ago, he and the chief administrative officer (CAO) had hoped that they could spur an improvement in the application and effectiveness of IT at the city. They were especially interested in making services available online to citizens, businesses, and visitors.

Three years later, the COO was frustrated by the lack of improvement in this area. At that time, the existing CIO retired. The COO decided to bring in an experienced CIO to thoroughly review the situation and make recommendations.

The new CIO quickly assessed that the IT department was doing a very good job of "keeping the lights on". Outages were few and were quickly resolved. The challenges in IT appeared to be more in the area of strategic improvement rather than day-to-day operations. He turned his focus beyond the IT department. He met with the department head of every department in the city. He asked them only three questions.

- What are your departmental objectives and challenges?
- How are you using information and communications technology?
- What do you think about IT?

He offered no answers, but probed to find out how IT looked in their eyes.

With minor exceptions, he found that departments were relatively happy with day-to-day systems. However, he found no consistent means of communication. There was a group within IT who were charged with managing the relationship between IT and the user departments. He found that this group was universally considered ineffective. When he asked about the impressions of IT, he was surprised to find that the responses he got were very inconsistent from department to department. One leader was effusive that he and his staff loved IT and that the people working there were great. Another angrily denounced the situation as intolerable. Some felt they got great support. Others referred to the relationship as adversarial. Several themes did emerge with some consistency.

- Departments never knew when any work they wanted would be done.
- They could not get advice from IT on how to meet their challenges.
- In an emergency, IT was always there when they were needed.

The CIO concluded that the organization was not getting the **value** from IT that it should. The municipality was looking to IT to transform the enterprise and was disappointed in the results.

To the CIO, this was not surprising. Transformation is not what IT was focused on. The last major system implementation was the deployment of an enterprise resource planning (ERP) system ten years before. Since then, all IT projects were focused on small systems, minor improvements, and technology life cycle.

How had the needs of the organizational leadership and the work of the IT department become so misaligned? A review of the work done by the group managing the relationship revealed the answer. The staff on this team in IT were relatively junior. They communicated with staff members in operational departments at an equally junior level. Collectively, these groups, relatively unaware of organizational objectives, put forward only minor requirements. No one was asking IT to do the big things. IT, being overwhelmed by so many little things, wasn't looking for more work.

This explained why some departments were happy and others not. Those that were focused solely on the tactical and day-to-day efforts were able to effectively work with IT. Those who looked for significant change could find no one in IT with whom to build a relationship.

The situation was exacerbated by the municipality's approach to budgeting and risk. Any large initiative, whether it involved technology or not, was usually broken down into many smaller components that were scheduled sequentially. This reduced risk and costs. That, in turn, made it more likely the work would be approved. Smart users realized that they shouldn't ask for big things but rather ask for one little piece of a big thing every year. This had the undesirable effect of pushing off any payback from projects much further out into the future.

Any IT project of significance in any organization will incur substantial expense at the beginning and may not show returns until several years later. Such projects are rarely completed within a single year. Their spending pattern tends to look like the following diagram Fig. 6.4 where the shaded area under the X axis represents a period of negative return and the shaded area above the X axis a positive one. For a good project, the latter will be larger than the former.

Due to the circumstances at the municipality, project spending and return tended to look like the diagram in Fig. 6.5. It was all investment and no return.

In other words, the city was spending the same amount per project, but over a longer period of time. However, they were never getting to the point where the major changes occurred that resulted in the big returns that would justify such expense.

On a larger scale, the same problem could be seen. Typically, an organization's spend on technology can be broken down into lights-on (run the business), enhancement/renewal (minor upgrades), and transformational (change

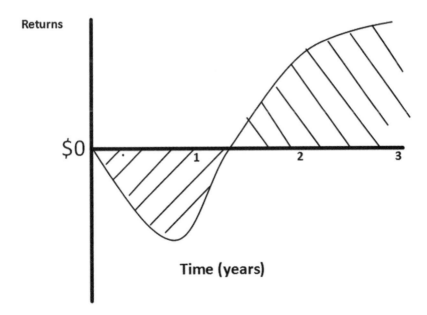

Fig. 6.4. Typical return curve for IT projects

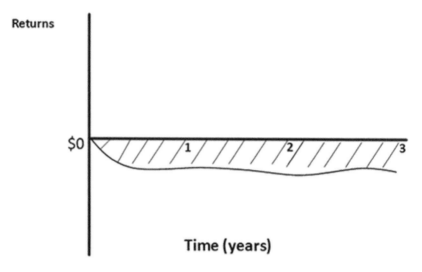

Fig. 6.5.   Impact on the return curve due to risk aversion

the business). Different authorities cite different numbers for an appropriate mix of these three types of work. For an organization as large and complex as a big municipality, a reasonable mix might be, percentage-wise, 70:20:10 for lights-on:enhancement/renewal:transformation. A portfolio analysis showed that the city was actually spending 80:20:0. Despite the fact that the COO and CAO had identified IT as a priority to meet serious challenges, nothing was being undertaken to truly transform the city's use of technology to make that happen.

The first recommendation that the CIO made was to change the mix of the portfolio to aggressively promote transformational projects and to significantly reduce the work being done for minor enhancements. To make up for years of lost time, it was recommended that, for the next three years, the portfolio mix of lights-on/enhancement or renewal/transformation be 70:10:20. This radical change would align the portfolio of work with the real needs of the city. The CIO also knew that in doing so, he would shift not only IT's focus but the entire organization's focus away from the details and toward the big picture. This recommendation was accepted.

The city council had set out a strategic plan in its first year in office. It was agreed that this plan would define the goals for transformational projects. The COO asked each department to review their current requests for work from IT and their future goals and rationalize it against these objectives.

These changes set a foundation on which to build. But they did not tell anyone what to build. What was needed was a clear plan. In the past, everything was open to change. There was no single view of the workload and no means to prioritize it. It was no wonder that departments complained that they never knew when they would get anything. IT never knew when it would deliver! Responsibility for the plan had to change from being IT's to being a corporate plan that was directing IT.

To achieve this corporate plan, proper governance was essential. It would be most common to start developing such a governance structure at the highest levels. However, the city represented a special challenge. Unlike an organization with a single objective such as a manufacturing business where departments are specialized, for instance, operations, sales, and marketing a city is made up of what is essentially separate businesses. The transit organization runs a completely separate operation from the social services department. Department heads, were in effect, CEOs of their organization.

A corporate governance team of department heads was established. This team was given the following mandate.

- Represent their department

    - Priorities
    - Understand implications
    - Communicate

- Be the corporate management team

    - One corporate plan for IT
    - Oversight

- Shepherd the plan through the budget process
- Be responsible for delivering value
- Share

    - Combine initiatives/requirements
    - Learn from each other

At the same time, the low-level relationship team within IT was reassigned. In its place, a beefed-up CIO's office with a few senior staff members was assigned to support the corporate governance team and manage the governance process on their behalf. This gave these busy people a support structure and a point of coordination. The CIO chaired this governance team.

The corporate governance team reported to the executive committee, a body that already existed and which included the COO and was chaired by the CAO. There was also an IT committee of council that had been formed to give political impetus to investment in technology. The plan would be presented to that committee for its approval, which would then take it to full council.

The second governance body was an architectural committee. This was chaired by the head of infrastructure support in IT and included technical representatives from different parts of IT and technical staff outside the IT department. Its responsibility was to ensure that the infrastructure was well-maintained and that the organization was making good architectural decisions. It reported to the corporate governance team.

A planning process was defined. This had to fit with the city's financial processes and had to mesh with the budgeting cycle. Since budgets went to council in the fall, the process was defined as follows:

- January–March—Input to planning process—assemble
  - Each department to prioritize its proposals
- April–May—Merge departmental plans into a corporate plan
  - Corporate governance team to prioritize all proposals received
- June–July—IT to present a draft plan to address priorities
- August—Draft plan recommended to corporate governance team
- September—Plan approved by corporate governance team
  - Included in budget from all departments
- October—finalization of plan in light of budget decisions
- November—Plan and budget presented to city council
- December—Final approved plan communicated broadly

This planning process had benefits that were attractive to management throughout the organization. The process was transparent. Every department would be involved in every step. With a completed and approved plan, there would be predictability that had previously been lacking. The content of the plan would be owned by the entire organization. The CIO would retain responsibility for the process of planning. A tie between the city strategic plan, the budget, and the IT plan would create alignment and facilitate decision making. Departments would get the information they needed to carry out their plans. IT would get the focus it needed to deliver on the right priorities.

While this was being implemented, IT did a thorough review of tits support and maintenance processes. These were reorganized to provide a clear means of communication and prioritization. Information Technology Infrastructure Library (ITIL) standards were employed to clearly differentiate between lights-on work and work that needed to be addressed through the new planning processes. In the review of the existing workload, a number of projects/requests already on the books were referred to the departments to address through the new planning process. Most of these did not pass their departmental prioritization process. By coupling the incoming requests with the goals and prioritization and making this visible to departmental management, a great deal of alignment was achieved.

Although the first implementation of the planning process had its challenges, it was carried through. The corporate management team became a strong governance body that kept the whole organization focused. This eased the burden on IT and allowed its staff to focus on a clearly defined set of priorities. Having to report to the corporate governance team also kept IT from losing its focus.

Metro City is now focused on getting real value from significant investments in IT to meet the serious challenges they face. They can plan, communicate, and provide oversight in ways that were not possible before. The IT department has clear objectives. While they are not easy, at least they are no longer moving targets. This enables them to apply their technical, support, and project management skills to greater effect than was possible in the past.

Governance can never be taken for granted. A regular review of the processes and effectiveness is something that each governance body will undertake on an annual basis. Like technology, continuous improvement should be a goal of governance as well.

Discussion Questions

1. Describe the IT governance arrangements in your organization. What are the key structural elements?
2. How is IT governance shaped by the IT services delivery model that prevails in your organization?
3. Discuss "IT governance takes place at all levels of the organization".
4. Illustrate, with an example, how timing plays a role in shaping how governance is approached.
5. What would you change about IT governance in your organization?

7

Enterprise Architecture

Good governance, as discussed in Chap. 6, requires more than a structure and regular meetings. There must be real communication. It is necessary to be able to effectively communicate plans, priorities, issues, and opportunities throughout the organization. This means having a coordinated view that ties together business and technical realities. It must allow nontechnical participants to understand the impact of technology as well as to let technologists understand the realities of business. To accomplish this, communication tools are needed. This chapter focuses on one of those tools—enterprise architecture (EA). Along with portfolio management (Chap. 8), these tools give everyone a coordinated view of what's happening in all the fields of the farm from the planting to the harvest and from the individual fields to the underlying infrastructure.

Enterprise Architecture

An EA is a living blueprint that articulates, in logical business and technical terms, the integrated relationship between business imperatives, business processes, information flows, information systems applications, and the technology and physical infrastructures that support the business in achieving its strategic objectives. It applies frameworks, models, standards, and tools to define the logical relationships and processes for ensuring effective and efficient coordination of resource and information flows, systems design and deployment, and project control and investment.

© The Editor(s) (if applicable) and The Author(s) 2016
G.G. Grant, R. Collins, *The Value Imperative*,
DOI 10.1057/978-1-137-59040-4_7

As a living document, it is regularly consulted, updated, and reviewed. It is a tool that is used constantly. It therefore, must have someone who is responsible for keeping it alive. As a blueprint, it must be thorough and must articulate both the individual aspects and their **integrated** relationships. It must be possible to understand cause and effect of a change in one aspect to other aspects of the blueprint. For example, if a change is made to the data collected at one point, it should be clear what impact that will have in other areas that use that data. Similarly, changes to the infrastructure should be traceable to the impacts they have on the systems, the business processes, and the ensuing business value (harvest). These are the relationships and processes that are at the heart of this tool.

EA is NOT a project. Although it is common to start a project to produce the first EA, there is a danger that the work stops when that first plan is produced. As Leon A. Kappleman said, "EA is more a *process* than a project; more a journey than a task. EA is an ongoing innovation and transformation initiative. It's about change in processes, procedures, and language. But, perhaps more importantly, it's about a change in the culture as well as the hearts and minds in the enterprise. EA is about big picture thinking, but is also about the little picture (in the context of the whole). It's about achieving balance in optimizing the whole and the parts, and therefore about the alignment of the whole and the parts"[1].

To achieve its purposes as a communications tool for a variety of people with different technical and business backgrounds, it is most useful to view an EA as having multiple layers. At the top is the business layer (Fig. 7.1). This is the most important layer as it includes the harvest of business value and the business processes that deliver that value. It is the primary starting point for people outside (and more often than not inside) the information technology (IT) organization. We strongly recommend that, when producing an EA, you start here. Too often, EA is started at the technology layer because that is where IT focuses. By starting at the business layer, it is possible (indeed it is necessary) to engage the rest of the organization in the EA. Also, as you progress down the layers, it will become obvious where the contents fit in the business context. (Or if it is not, it identifies a problem that requires urgent attention.) Most important, starting with business keeps the focus on the harvest and this will continue throughout the effort, ensuring that EA will be a useful communication tool.

---

[1] Kappelman, L. A. (ed.) (2009) Chapter 3: Enterprise Architecture Practice—The SIM Guide to Enterprise Architecture, Auerbach Publications.

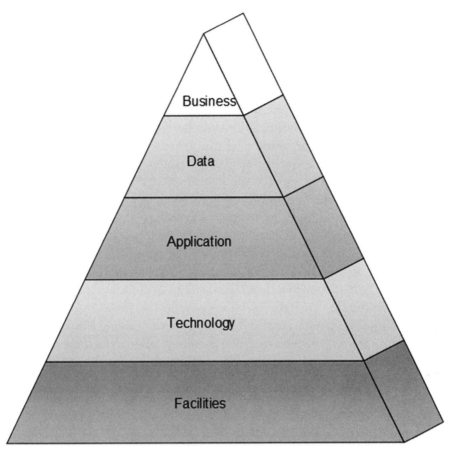

Fig. 7.1 Enterprise architecture—a layered view

Below the business layer is the data layer. This data architecture is vital to understanding how information is communicated (or not) throughout an organization. It will show transactional data as well as data formatted for decision support. It will highlight where information is not coordinated or duplicated. The data layer provides the most opportunity for information asymmetry to occur. Asymmetry is prevalent at this layer because organizations often acquire and store data over long periods. Fragmentation of data stores and data flows create disconnects that restrict the ability to easily access and share data across the organization.

Below the data layer is the application layer. The application layer comprises the software systems and processes that specify how the business and functional relationships are instantiated. Application systems enable business process execution, integrating functional and enterprise data, functional application systems, middleware, and other system functionalities. The application layer is the province of significant IT investments. It is here that business executives focus much of their IT investment effort because of how applications enable the processes that executives care about.

Below the application layer is the technology layer. It is here that we see the specific pieces of technology and the various sources for them. This technology will include software, hardware, and networks, among others, and comprise both in-house and extraorganizational components Part of this layer should include the maintenance and currency of technology components (e.g., how up-to-date are they on versions of application software).

The final layer is the facilities layer. Too often this is forgotten. However, knowing where everything is located is vital to such processes as business continuity planning and risk management. Often, facilities are not included in discussion of architecture. They are assumed to be available. However, as experience from major disasters, such as Hurricane Katrina in 2005 or the 1997 ice storm in Eastern Canada, demonstrate, considerations of physical facilities and their location is vital. Many lives were lost in New Orleans through systems failures because servers and equipment were located in lower-level areas, such as building basements, when the city was flooded. Given that New Orleans is below sea level, a greater focus on the physical architecture would have suggested to executives and technical people that equipment should be located at higher levels and that off-site business continuity repositories should have been included in the technical mix.

Taking a layered view of EA provides at least two benefits. One, it illustrates the interconnected and integrated view of the enterprise and its component parts. It demonstrates the dependencies that exist between the various parts of the enterprise and shows the effects of changes in any one part on the other part. The second significant benefit is that it allows for in-depth and detailed discussion and treatment of the individual components without having to have detailed and expert knowledge of all the other components and layers (an idea called "encapsulation" in other settings). This means, for example, that business managers can describe and express their business needs without having to be experts on the technicalities of servers and networks. Encapsulation, as in the case for designing buildings or telecommunication networks, allows each expert group to design, select, and acquire the best components for delivering on the ultimate goal, the harvest (i.e., the business value that the customer is willing to pay for). Too often, business executives and non-IT people want to dictate how a particular business requirement is designed and delivered without a good understanding of the implications. Some go as far as shutting out IT people from technology acquisition discussions, a practice often promoted by organizations seeking to sell technology to business leaders. Without appropriate background, business leaders are lured into buying decisions that later come back to haunt them because they did not fully understand the technical implications of the decisions they were making.

It is best for there to be two states in the EA—"as is" and "to be." The former represents the state of the farm as it exists today. The latter represents the desired state of the farm to be achieved in the future. This temporal view of the EA allows people to understand the goals and make detailed plans in context of broader objectives and circumstances.

A Layered Architecture View for Governing IT Service Delivery Investments

Often, discussions of IT service delivery investments devolve into a confused jumble of ideas about business demands, technical specificities, and governance and management concerns. For example, a business decision to implement an enterprise resource planning (ERP) system rapidly descends into a discussion of a specific ERP offering and technical details about the database and operating systems. Such discussions often lead to conflicts, which are avoidable if addressed from the point of view of a layered architecture.

Figure 7.2, outlines one way of discussing and communicating ideas about IT service delivery investments and management. It can be used to frame the issues that must be addressed when making decisions about IT investments. As well, it serves to encapsulate the issues being discussed so that each issue can be addressed appropriately without losing connection to the integrated whole. So, for example, if an organization, whether through previous disjointed efforts or through the fact that many recent acquisitions have been made, finds itself with a vast array of incompatible and disjointed IT infrastructure and applications, it can use this framework to carefully analyze, discuss, and take action to streamline the investments that need to be made to bring about a well-functioning and integrated IT landscape. The framework has three main areas of concern: governance and planning; required services; and service delivery, management, and evaluation. The governance and planning section focuses on who is accountable for what decisions about IT investments. Accountability begins with the corporate board, which is responsible for setting overall vision, policy, direction, and authority for all decisions about investments in IT services and systems. Without the strong guidance of the board, IT decisions can easily become disconnected from the overall goals and objectives of the organization. Many boards pay little attention to IT issues

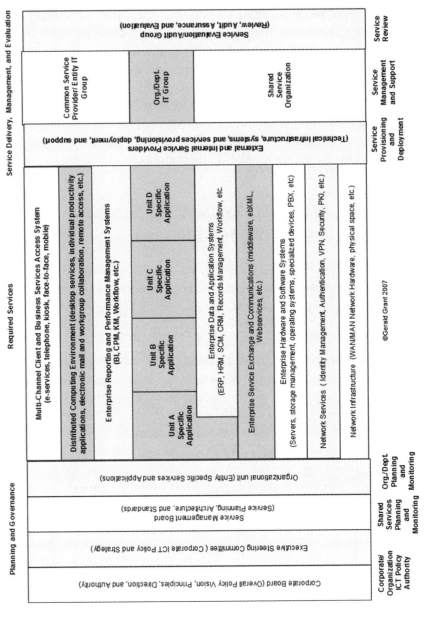

Fig. 7.2. An example of a high-level architecture for IT services management

or give them cursory overviews. Such a lack of attention from the pinnacle of governance can have serious repercussions such as those cited in *Fortune Magazine*[2] in 2014. They listed breaches at some of the top companies in the

---

[2] Fortune.com/2014/10/03/5-huge-cybersecurity-breakins-at-big-companies/

world including Wal-Mart, Home Depot, Target, Apple, Nieman Marcus, and J. P. Morgan. In some cases, costs were estimated in the millions of dollars. In all, the reputation of companies was harmed. The board must set the direction and tone for the rest of the organization to follow.

Executive management through various governance bodies and mechanisms set IT policy and strategy and make decisions on the portfolio of IT investments. Often executive management abdicate this responsibility and depend on business groups to make these decisions. However, doing this can only lead to fragmented services and systems and duplicated investments. Executive management must go beyond "rubber stamping" decisions made at lower levels of the organizations and must engage actively in strategy-setting and portfolio management activities. This will give focus to organizational priorities and enable operational alignment with organizational goals.

Service management boards are responsible for service planning and strategy and for setting and monitoring service architecture requirements and standards. These boards give oversight to common and shared service arrangements, ensuring that service requirements are met. In some contexts, service operations may need to be run at the organization or department level to give focus to specific and unique local application requirements. Such local service operations must represent a deliberate choice by the organization as a whole. It should not be simply a rogue operation by individual managers to avoid the scrutiny of the larger organization. Allowing such rogue operations will sow the seeds for future chaos.

Adopting a layered architecture view of required IT services is the key to understanding how to effectively deliver those services to the organization and its customers. Every higher-level service is dependent on the effective execution of a lower-level service. Each service has its own requirements and parameters for service execution and connection with other services. Delivery of a higher-level service is supported and constrained by the characteristics of the lower-level service on which it depends. We illustrate this with an example of an airline passenger acquiring a boarding pass.

At the highest level, the service that customers require is access to a boarding pass that will allow them to board an airplane. There are multiple channels for accessing the application that will generate the boarding pass. Customers can access the application through their own personal computer at home, through their mobile devices, at a kiosk in the airport, or after waiting in a long line for the airline employee at the counter to generate the boarding pass for them. Any of these channels, when used, will have certain affordances and constraints. Using a mobile device allows for great flexibility and removes the constraint of going to an actual counter at the airport to get a boarding pass. However, a customer may find that receiving an electronic boarding pass that may not be accepted on some flight segments.

Being able to access the electronic boarding pass service on multiple channels is dependent on a distributed computing service environment providing remote application access. The applications allow for the presentation of customer information generated by a variety of reporting systems. These systems draw on enterprise data contained in ERP, CRM, and other data management systems. Connections between enterprise hardware and software systems are facilitated by various service exchange and communications protocols. Enterprise hardware and software systems depend on a host of network services for systems access and authentication. These networks services are deployed on network infrastructure that are foundational to information availability and sharing. All of these are housed in physical infrastructures built to contain the tangible IT artifacts.

Often, some departments feel strongly that they have unique applications that must be dealt with outside the services architecture of the organization in which they reside. They may cite unique processes or clientele that must be served in unique ways. Consequently, they demand their own infrastructure investments. The extent to which this is true must always be tested. What aspect of the service requirement is unique? Is the uniqueness at the applications layer or at the infrastructure layer? For example, having a requirement for a different server doesn't mean going out and buying a different physical machine. Servers can be provisioned virtually and may run on a single physical machine. Similarly, requiring a different application doesn't mean having a separate database. Different applications can use the same underlying data. So asking the question, "what is unique", is vital in making IT investment decisions.

Note that in describing the required services, no effort was made to prescribe how they are manifested, delivered, or paid for. This is because each service, though necessary, can be delivered in a multitude of ways, each approach having benefits and drawbacks. Currently, for example, many services can be provisioned as cloud-based services without any investment in physical assets except the interface device. Cloud-based services are not a panacea and may not be appropriate for some situations. Sometimes these services are delivered as common services or through shared services arrangements. In special cases, individual units or departments may act as service providers. Options for sourcing services should not be conflated with the service requirements discussion. Even if a shared services organization or department is accountable for delivering certain services, it may, instead of developing its own capacity locally, source the services from the market through other providers thus separating the accountability from the delivery mechanism.

Finally, all service delivery plans and arrangements need to be evaluated and audited to ensure performance and compliance with requirements, policy, regulations, and laws. This service review is critical to the investment decision cycle. Successful investments may draw further investments. Audits may highlight compliance gaps and potential risk factors. In the TJX[3] security breach case,[4] a more thorough audit might have highlighted the potential risk of not complying with the security requirements for credit card processing.

The layered architecture view for IT service delivery is a particularly useful tool for improving the communications and discourse about IT investments by organizations. It allows for more fruitful interchange because governance issues, service requirements, and delivery options are discussed in the appropriate space. No longer should service requirement discussion be unnecessarily conflated with service delivery options or service governance options be held hostage by the physical requirements of IT infrastructure. Each aspect can be addressed fully in an encapsulated way.

When to Use the Enterprise Architecture

The EA should be consulted for every decision to be made about IT systems. Only by doing so will decisions be kept in context of the greater plans. Equally, only by doing so will the EA be kept current.

The EA should also be used when making investment decisions. The "to be" state should reflect the long-term plans and, from these plans, candidates for investment brought forward. Not only does the EA help to determine where to invest, but it also shows where NOT to invest. If a system in the "as is" architecture is slated to be replaced in the "to be" architecture, then investments, large or small, in that system are unlikely to pay back as they will not have the time to do so.

The EA is also key to maintaining and updating the infrastructure. By showing the impact of decisions made elsewhere on the underlying infrastructure, the EA can help business leaders understand the need for investment in technology not directly related to a specific business process. Again, the "to be" and "as is" states of the EA can be especially effective in putting forward investment plans for infrastructure.

---

[3] Computer world, March 29, 2007 http://www.computerworld.com/article/2544306/security0/tjx-data-breach--at-45-6m-card-numbers--it-s-the-biggest-ever.html

[4] Evers, J. (2007) T. J. Maxx hack exposes consumer data, C|Net, February 21, accessed April 30, 2016 at http://www.cnet.com/news/t-j-maxx-hack-exposes-consumer-data/

Benefits of EA

Once you have an EA, you can use it to facilitate planning and communication throughout the organization. It will produce the following benefits.

- It will bring together business and technical complexity allowing them to be discussed and managed in a coordinated fashion.
- It will make it clear how the technology impacts the business and how the business impacts the technology.
- It will shift the focus from technical efficiency to business value.
- By providing frameworks, processes, and tools for dealing with complexity and uncertainty in applying technologies, it will support organizational and business objectives.
- It will outline a vision of the future.
- It will improve morale as more individuals see a direct correlation between their work and the organization's success.
- It will create a common language for communication between the business and technical stakeholders.

These benefits highlight the fact that the EA is a communications tool. It is not a blueprint for technologists. It is the basis of understanding across the organization both in breadth (multiple departments) and in depth (executive management to computer room).

Don't Boil the Ocean

A great value of a good EA is that it covers the breadth and depth of the entire organization. This is also one of the greatest challenges in developing an EA. It can take significant time to document everything. If nothing is done to provide benefit during that time, then patience (and money) often runs out before the work is completed.

Rather than set out to create the ultimate EA, it is better to start with a specific problem. This must be a problem that deals with more than one system and the interrelationships and competing pressures of some subset of the entire IT farm. For the first iteration of an EA, develop only the pieces needed to deal with this specific situation. Acknowledge, up front, that there will be more work to do later, but define the boundaries and stay within them.

This will reduce the time it takes to produce a usable result. By choosing a pressing issue, it will be easier to engage nontechnical parts of the organization to get involved. It will be possible to explain the benefit and the time to see that the benefit will be compelling. This not only will allow an organization to create the communication tools to address a specific problem but will hone the skills of those involved. If this first iteration is successful, it will create an appetite for a larger EA.

This iterative approach can be most successful in organizations that do not have an institutional bent toward strong documentation. (This is most of the organizations in the world.) Just as we want IT systems to focus on value, so the EA exercise should also focus on a harvest. One good harvest will lead to many more.

Maintaining an Enterprise Architecture

Too often EA is regarded as a technical tool. While it should, at its lowest level, delve to the technical depths of the organization, that should not be the focus. An EA is a communication vehicle. It is not solely for IT technical staff. It is a tool that should be used across the entire organization, both in breadth and depth. To do this, it must articulate how the IT systems impact everyone. It cannot be just about "feeds and speeds". It must speak to business processes and business value.

Unsurprisingly, the key here is to communicate the harvest. By ensuring that this business value is at the heart of the EA, organizations can ensure that this tool will be useful to all. When done well, EA gives a sense of common ownership. To do this, it is necessary for the IT organization to recognize that the systems belong to various departments or the organization as a whole, not to IT. By communicating this sense of ownership, the enterprise architecture also conveys a sense of responsibility. Ideally, this will also be reflected in the organizational governance. EA is a tool that should be familiar to all in the governance process.

An EA is not a static document. Too often, once completed, the architecture is put on the shelf and quickly becomes out of date. It must be a living document that is updated when there is any change to IT systems or to the processes supported by those systems. As a map of the IT farm, it is necessary to reflect the conditions today, not in the past. And, as a communications vehicle, it is important to review the document regularly so that people are aware of the changing state of the farm.

The temporal change must also be reflected. As work is undertaken to move from the "as is" architecture to the "to be" state, this must be reflected in the

EA. As decisions are made about investments, the EA should be updated. In this way, all projects and systems can stay abreast of changes that may impact them.

National Department Stores—EA as a Communications Tool[5]

National Department Stores is a chain of stores that started in New York in the 1920s and has spread across North America and into Europe and the Caribbean. Its traditional business model had been seriously impacted by online shopping. To compete, it had made the movement to online sales a major goal. This seemed an effort that everyone could agree on. So it was surprising that after a year, not a single sale had taken place on the Internet. When the COO investigated this, he discovered that IT was spending all of its time researching and planning significant investment in its infrastructure. Yet IT could not explain how this investment would achieve the goal nor why it was important enough to hold up the shifting of sales online.

To address this issue, the COO created an IT function within the sales department. The COO knew that he could count on the management here to focus on the goal of revenue and not get caught up in a lot of technology. The responsibility for online sales was transferred from Central IT to this new group.

A year later, things had progressed no further. The new IT group in Sales had come up with a number of plans and ideas, some of which had been prototyped. But none of them had gone into production. That group blamed Central IT for being unresponsive. Central IT responded that the requirements from this group were vague and unrealistic. The COO was disappointed to learn that, even though he had set up a group with a specific focus, they continued to look for changes to existing systems and large efforts in underlying technology. Why couldn't people just get something done?

Within the central IT department, there was a small group that was developing an EA. They had researched what was needed for a complete EA and had attended courses and conferences to learn best practices. They were engaged in an exercise that had been going on for almost two years. By their estimates, they had documented 20% of the complex infrastructure and systems of National Department Stores. This group's work, while expected to be the backbone of IT's strategy, was influencing nothing at all.

---

[5] This example draws on the experience of several real-world organizations and is designed to illustrate EA's value as a communication tool.

The chief information officer (CIO) gave the EA group a new mandate. Stop trying to document everything and just focus solely on the issues arising in the efforts to move sales online. They were to report to the IT manager in the sales department and enable her to explain exactly what the relationship was between online sales and existing systems. They had a deadline of three months. The EA group protested that this would only give a partial picture and was not consistent with what they had learned of best practices. The CIO was unmoved.

Embracing their new mandate, the EA group dove into the challenges facing the sales group. They interviewed everyone and began drawing diagrams from the business processes on down rather than from the technology up as they had been proceeding. This was the only way they could find to connect to the people in Sales and the stores who seemed to have no interest in the big picture of technology and infrastructure.

Once they had documented what Sales wanted to do, which they called the "to be" diagram, they documented the existing systems that provided the in-store systems today, which they called the "as is" diagram. They then presented this to the sales group, pointing out where it was going to be necessary to bridge the gap between the "to be" and "as is" models.

The Sales IT manager referred to this as the greatest breakthrough she had seen in two years. For the first time, she truly understood the job before her. As a nontechnical, revenue-oriented leader, she had struggled to break through the techno-babble coming from IT people in her own department as well as the Central IT department. Now she could map it out herself in two clear, concise diagrams. While she was slightly daunted by the challenge she now understood, she was buoyed by being able to fully articulate that challenge in terms that made sense to her, her department, and her management. She directed her team to put together a rollout plan using the EA diagrams as the basis of the communication.

The Sales VP then took this plan to the COO. Within fifteen minutes, he finally had the answer to his questions of how hard it was and what it would take to get the job done. He approved the plan put forward and communicated it as a priority to all departments including Central IT. The Sales VP and the CIO communicated the plan to a joint session of both departments and clarified responsibilities and priorities to everyone. The bulk of the presentation consisted of the two EA diagrams.

As work progressed to details, the EA grew. Wherever there was a need to coordinate, the EA expanded to provide the details. Unlike previous experience, where managers were loath to commit effort to the EA project, there was now a demand to be allowed to participate in the EA.

As predicted by the EA team, the limited EA suffered from a lack of thoroughness. Systems and technologies that had not been included suddenly needed to be added as plans firmed up. But, rather than this being a problem, it was a boon to the team. The EA grew as questions were asked by people from outside the EA team. It might not be the formulaic approach that they would have preferred but, by responding to demand, they were making progress in documenting the entire architecture at a pace that vastly surpassed their two previous years of work.

The EA became a cornerstone of governance as well as of system design. It was referenced at all levels including executive management. The connection between the service being provided (business process) and the underlying systems made it clear why work was being done, money being spent, and how it was all coming together to achieve the goals of the organization. By focusing on the organization's most pressing challenge, the EA team brought the organization together with a common understanding and language. In return, the success of the EA in this limited role led to a demand to develop the full EA from the very people who had balked at participating in the past.

Discussion Questions

1. Does your organization have an EA?
2. How and when is it used? By whom?
3. How might it better serve communication in your organization?
4. Use the layered architecture view for IT service delivery to assess your organization's IT services governance, requirements, and delivery approaches.

8

IT Investment Portfolio

As discussed in Chap. 6, good governance is necessary to ensure that real business value is being created by investments in information technology (IT). Effective communication is fundamental to good governance. Chapter 7 discussed one primary tool of communication—enterprise architecture (EA). In this chapter, we will discuss another communication tool that we have found to be extremely effective—the IT investment portfolio. Together, these communication tools will provide a strong underpinning for good governance that will vastly increase the likelihood that investments produce real value.

IT portfolio management is a significant vehicle for decision making and communications about IT investments in organizations. Just as a wealth investment manager tracks a wide variety of assets that produce certain returns, so IT is responsible for a set of assets that, in different ways, are intended to produce business value for the organization.

IT portfolio management is a disciplined method of managing IT investments in organizations. This does not just apply to new investments, but accounts for the myriad of legacy investments made in the past for which IT is responsible. It provides a means to balance both the risks and the rewards of IT investments. It increases transparency around decisions about IT investments. As well, IT portfolio management communicates organizational priorities—both business and technical.

As Bryan Maizlish and Robert Handler said in 2005, IT portfolio management "provides the tools, processes, and disciplines needed to translate information technology into a common taxonomy that both business and IT

© The Editor(s) (if applicable) and The Author(s) 2016
G.G. Grant, R. Collins, *The Value Imperative*,
DOI 10.1057/978-1-137-59040-4_8

executives understand…"[1] If this sounds similar to what was said about EA, it is. Both of these tools work to provide the communication vehicle needed to manage the IT farm and reap the harvest. They work together, providing different views of the same things.

Good portfolio management will foster strategic business and IT alignment. It will result in strategic investments and better returns on those investments. It not only deals with investments made but also recognizes that the resources used to make that investment are no longer available to be invested elsewhere. (A field planted with corn is no longer available to plant wheat.) It also recognizes that past investments shape decisions for future investments. (e.g., enterprise resource planning [ERP] will continue to require the commitment of resources after it has gone into production.) Legacy infrastructure, for instance, is difficult to uproot and change. Consequently, new investments are likely to be constrained by the capabilities and features of assets obtained earlier. This suggests that there is always a path-dependent relationship between decisions made in the past and those made later. It means then that business and IT executives must be careful and prescient in the investment choices made, to avoid being saddled with investments that can hamper future efforts.

Maizlish and Handler outline a very practical way of visualizing IT investment options and the risk and return relationship (Fig. 8.1). This is a common model used in IT portfolio management. It can be adapted to fit the specifics of any organization. It shows that organizations spend a certain percentage of their IT budget (money, staff, and resources) to run the business. This is often referred to as keeping the lights on. The spending is on core infrastructure and nondiscretionary services and systems. It includes core functions such as networks, storage, security, communications, and nondiscretionary expenses such as those needed to keep existing applications functional and efficient. This is the primary responsibility of IT. Spending on this type of IT will usually run in the range of 60 %–70 % of available budget capacity. The more complex the organization, the higher the percentage is likely to be. However, a high percentage does not necessarily point to greater complexity. It may simply reflect a poorly integrated legacy of expensive systems suffering from a lack of maintenance and renewal.

Executive management often forget that "run the business" expenses are both necessary and key to business survival. They are likely to be interested in funding new projects to the neglect of less-visible IT requirements. Too often, core IT infrastructure is neglected because there are no business cham-

---

[1] Maizlish, B. and Handler, R. (2005) IT portfolio management: step-by-step, Hoboken, NJ, John Wiley and Sons, p. 4.

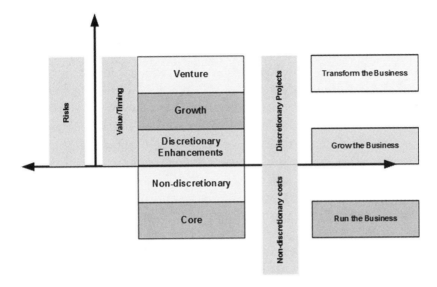

Fig. 8.1.   IT investment portfolio classifications
Source: Maizlish and Handler 2005, p. 205

pions for it. It is incumbent of IT leaders to ensure that a business case is made for core IT infrastructure investments. Business leaders must be led to understand that superior business value cannot emerge from a faulty and weak IT platform. IT infrastructure that is disjointed, incompatible, insecure, and fragile will be a disaster waiting to happen. Investment in infrastructure renewal on a recurring cycle is good practice for all organizations seeking to derive substantial business value.

Classifying IT Investment Portfolios

Another tranche of resources will be spent to grow the business. This includes minor enhancements that need to occur in the natural growth of the organization. This reflects business continuity and the small, continuous improvement of existing business processes. Additional investments focused on expanding the business are also included here. These represent strategic investments that build the capacity of the business to expand its markets and reach new customers. Investments made in services, systems, and human capacity are crucial to business growth. Depending upon the situation in any organization, from 10 % to 30 % can be spent here. The more stable the business and marketplace in which it operates, the higher this is likely to be.

At the upper level, we have investment that may generate significant change to the organization. These are likely new ventures that represent innovations that are intended to significantly change the business and its processes. They are (or should be) tied to strategic goals of the organization. Such investments are likely to carry a great deal more risk than other investments, but are also more likely, if successful, to deliver extraordinary value. Venture investments usually amount to between 5 % and 10 % of available budget unless there is a serious threat to the organization, when it is likely to be more. It is important to note that most organizations have a limited scope to absorb significant and constant change. Prudent management will be very selective in the venture investments pursued as organizations can only consume so much change (business as well as IT) at any one time.

This portfolio diagram gives a good big-picture visualization of how money and resources are being spent within the context of organizational operations. It is a great communications device. It does not contain details about specific projects or systems, but rather outlines the key options for investments that the business has. It is an excellent model to explain how an organization has decided to commit its assets and is often the first view presented in a review of an organization's overall portfolio.

Visualizing IT Portfolio Risk/Reward

Rarely does one view of the portfolio suffice. Another view that can communicate complex ideas in an easy-to-grasp format is outlined in Fig. 8.2.

This commonly used portfolio view showcases the types, relative size and cost of investment, and potential for contributing to business profitability. Vertical positioning in the quadrants also indicates the probability of technical success on the investment option. The quadrants are then used to classify specific assets in the portfolio. In this example, the upper-right quadrant, entitled Bread and Butter, contains the assets that run the business. They embody the substantive cost outlay and provide a low to moderate return to the organization. It would be common to find ERP systems and other similar operating platforms in this quadrant. These types of operational systems are candidates for regular improvement and cost management but not for radical change (unless this is an initial implementation).

The lower-right quadrant contains White Elephants. These are assets that cost a great deal and are likely to be technical and organizational failures. They cost a lot of money and will be a drain on resources without much

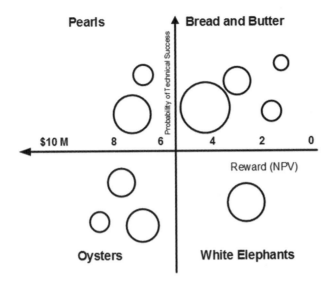

Adapted from Cooper, R. G., Edgett, S. J., and Klienschmidt, E. J. (2001) Portfolio Management for New Products, Perseus Publishing.

Fig. 8.2.   Portfolio view of IT investments and their contribution

possibility of producing a return. These are candidates for replacement or even elimination. By removing the White Elephants, resources can be reallocated to more beneficial assets or new ventures. Systems classified as White Elephants are most likely to be older legacy systems that often escape regular review by virtue of their heritage but which have come, over time, to produce a poor harvest.

In the upper left are the Pearls. These take fewer resources to manage and maintain but produce a high reward. These may include applications such as business intelligence systems or assets used by a specific department for a specific initiative. This is an area to look for potential to replicate the success in other areas of the organization.

Finally, the lower left contains the Oysters. These are systems that may become Pearls but haven't reached their full potential yet. They may be systems recently deployed or experiments in new technology. These should be watched carefully (nurtured and cultivated) to determine if they are going to become Pearls, Bread and Butter, or White Elephants.

Other quadrant views can be very useful for identifying information asymmetry and redundancy. A quadrant showing applications against data sets and user communities can easily highlight where different parts of the organization are using different data to understand what should be the same information. It can also show where multiple systems are being used to do essentially the same job. Using the IT farm analogy would show where multiple fields are being employed to produce multiple harvests where only one harvest is needed.

These quadrant views of the portfolio are excellent tools for the renewal phase of the Value Realization Cycle (VRC). They show where investments are paying off and where they are not. They may also show where resources are being stretched and where, despite the value of each individual asset, the underlying infrastructure and staffing are being put under pressure to keep the lights on.

Evaluating the Portfolio

There are different ways to evaluate the overall portfolio of technology investments. Often the decision on how to evaluate will have more to do with the maturity of an organization than with the technologies involved. For example, an organization that has rigorous standards for fiscal management, such as a bank, would be able to use hard and fast measurement of dollars to make decisions. On the other hand, an organization that is just starting to grow into this type of management may lack the rigor and would be better served by a more subjective assessment of its portfolio.

Subjective measures can be as simple as "high/medium/low" for value and cost and "red/yellow/green" for status. For organizations new to portfolio management, it can be a quick and easy way to start. As the organization delves into specifics or becomes more sophisticated, this subjective measure will give way to harder metrics.

Better results may be achieved with more objective evaluations, though this is no guarantee that the right allocation of resources is being made. Such evaluations require that the organization have some standards for objective measurement and the processes to make those measurements. Numeric measures are most common, with monetary units (dollars, Euros, Yens, etc.) being the most likely, but by no means the only, values to be measured. Objective evaluation is necessary for larger portfolios and for the ability to track investments and results after decisions have been made. However, care must be taken to ensure that the focus remains on the business value (harvest) and that detailed metrics do not deviate from or overwhelm the larger business sense.

Over time, the goal is to optimize the model. This will differ depending upon the state of the organization and the environment in which it operates. Just as personal investment portfolios change as people move from higher earning years toward retirement, so the correct mix of an organization's technology investments will change over time. If an organization is facing a critical problem or opportunity, its appetite for risk will be higher. If it is in a mature state, the appetite for risk will be much lower.

No one view is enough to manage a portfolio. Different aspects of the technology and business as well as the metrics to be evaluated require multiple lenses, or views, of the portfolio. There is no magic formula to add up the numbers and come to a conclusion. Portfolio management requires significant effort and managerial judgement to evolve and assess models.

Portfolio Management Is the Renewal Phase

In the VRC, there is a renewal phase that looks at the big picture and assesses it against the broad strategic objectives of the organization. This not only analyzes the results across all the systems but also creates input to the evolution of strategic goals.

An annual review of the entire IT farm is part of the governance process. Using a number of portfolio lenses, IT can communicate the health of all the systems in context. Here major issues can be raised. It is through this process that IT can most effectively put forward those large technology investment options, such as network upgrades, that are so difficult to justify against individual projects.

A good example of this is the backlog of legacy systems. It is notoriously difficult to deal with the legacy of applications and tools that have built up over the years. A governance review of the legacy provides exactly the means to do that. The status and health of each system can be communicated with its incumbent costs and its annual harvest. But, perhaps more important, the sum of those costs can also be communicated. That 60 %–70 % of IT's efforts spent keeping the lights on warrants at least as much review and oversight as the 30 %–40 % of the effort dedicated to bring about small or large changes.

This can be especially useful during periods of pressure on IT. As systems grow beyond the growth in resources to support them, a portfolio review can quickly communicate the pressure being created, the potential impact of such pressure, and the alternatives to dealing with that pressure. It is here that IT can validly put forward the options of eliminating some older systems. It is also in this context that IT can most effectively deal with sourcing options (see Chap. 9).

The renewal phase is vital to the health of an organization's technological infrastructure. Portfolio management provides an effective and efficient tool to communicate this to the entire organization.

Heldon Industrial—Using Portfolio to Understand and Communicate[2]

Heldon Industrial was a conglomerate of mining and manufacturing operations on four continents. It had grown through acquisition and regularly acquired new companies or divested existing holdings. Each holding operated relatively independently. This made it easier to bring on new acquisitions or sell off existing ones. Economies of scale were focused on the back offices' functions including HR, Finance, and IT, which were centralized.

Heldon Industrial was not satisfied with its efforts to apply technology to strategic problems. The IT department was clearly overworked, and everyone had demands that were piling up. How could it be that IT was being successful at neither the strategic nor the tactical challenges that it faced?

The first hurdle in analyzing this problem was that there was no clear, single source of information to explain what IT was doing. Consistent with the culture of such a diverse organization, IT had developed a close relationship with all of the subsidiaries it served by adapting its processes to those of its user communities. The problem was that each subsidiary operated in a different fashion. This is not surprising. Running a mining organization requires very different processes from manufacturing steel or transoceanic shipping. In its search for alignment, IT had developed different processes and communication vehicles for each subsidiary or department. This meant that no one had a handle on the big picture. There was no single list of ongoing projects or existing systems. There was no common definition of priorities nor was there any consistent means of assessing the value of any effort. Each system was dealt with in isolation of all others. When this is the case, all work is justifiable and it is difficult to make choices from a variety of options. Thus, IT was overwhelmed.

The lack of progress against the strategic goals of the organization was identified as the primary issue. A review was done of all the work being undertaken or in any backlog list, and it was classified as one of the following:

- Lights on
  - Work being done to carry on business as usual
- Continuous improvement

  - Work on existing systems to address specific issues or make minor changes but not addressing changes to business processes or having a measurable impact on the organization's strategic goals
  - Regularly scheduled technology life cycle renewal

---

[2] This example draws on the experience of several real-world organizations and is designed to illustrate the value of IT portfolio management as a communication tool.

- Transformational change

  - Work targeted directly at measurable change to achieve the organization's strategic goals

To get everything assessed, it was necessary to interview every team in IT and review their individual lists of work and then confirm these lists with each subsidiary or department. The result showed that almost four-fifths of IT's effort was "lights on" work and that all of the remainder was "continuous improvement." No effort was being focused on transformational change. This conclusion was communicated by the chief information officer (CIO) to executive management. Their initial reaction was that IT was working on the wrong things. However, because they had done their homework in advance, IT was able to show how it was responding to exactly what was being asked of it by the various parts of the corporation. It was not that IT was working on the wrong things. It was that IT was being asked to work on the wrong things and wasn't being asked to work on the organizational priorities. There was alignment with each subsidiary and department, but there was no alignment across these entities and no alignment to the strategic objectives of the corporation.

With just this limited portfolio view, it was possible to shift the conversation from one focused on IT's failings to one focused on the entire organization's priorities. The failure of communication and focus was found to be not, as expected, between IT and the various corporate components, but within every subsidiary and department (including IT) and between the executive levels and the day-to-day managers responsible for exploiting IT. The CIO worked with the CEO and the various executive heads to propose an alternative, or target portfolio, that would shift much of the effort toward the strategic priorities. Several projects were identified as high-value, strategic efforts that could be started immediately. This target portfolio was approved by the executive committee.

The next step was to address the existing portfolio to make room for the new work. It was estimated that these strategic initiatives would take 20 % of IT's efforts. Where was that 20 % to come from? It was unrealistic to expect an increase in the IT budget of 20 %. Therefore, the existing portfolio had to be reduced by that amount. The work to explain the existing portfolio paid off again when the CIO was able to use it to communicate to the rest of the executives that they had to participate in reducing their demand to make room for the approved plan.

Departments defended their priority by classifying it as "lights-on" requirements. The CIO knew that this was not truly the case. IT came up with a clear definition for "lights-on" work that provided another portfolio view that helped all departments understand the objectives and adjust their priorities. Lights-on work was defined into four categories, based on the Information Technology Infrastructure Library(ITIL) model. These included:

- Break/fix
  - This is any problem where the system used to work but does not work now. This includes maintenance to prevent failures.
- Natural growth
  - Support for "more of the same." This included work where additional operations or services were added that used exactly the same business model and systems as existing services. For example—a new mine being run in the same fashion as existing mines.
- Technology life cycle
  - The regular update of existing technology to prevent failures in the future (e.g., upgrading from Windows XP to Windows 7 before XP expired).
- Service requests
  - Response to calls to the help desk using a defined service catalog that was made broadly available on the corporate intranet.

This second portfolio view reassured management that IT was focusing on keeping the organization running. It also was fundamental to the discussions to severely pare down the large list of minor enhancement projects that made up the bulk of the backlog. Subsidiaries and departments were left with a list of past requirements that fit neither into the lights-on nor the strategic portfolios. These had to be reviewed and prioritized relative to the limited resources assigned to minor enhancements. Each subsidiary and department reviewed their list and eliminated many of them. The remainder were then prioritized by the corporate governance team.

These two simple portfolio views underpinned a significant transformation not only of IT's workload but of its position within the organization and its relationships with all of the functions it supported.

Communications Tools

EA and IT portfolio management are two of the best tools to enable communication and support decision making within an organization. When developing these tools, it is vital to keep the focus on the business value. These are tools for the whole organization, not just IT. They give an organization the view of the farm, an assessment of the harvest, and its commensurate cost.

Such tools are living documents. They must be kept up-to-date and reflect the constant change of any organization. As such, there must be someone responsible to do this. It is easy to set aside such responsibilities in times of difficulty. However, a lack of attention to these tools will result in a loss of alignment within the organization, an inability to make key decisions, and potentially significant failure of the IT underpinning any organization.

Discussion Questions

1. Can you assess the systems used by a particular business function in your organization using the portfolio models outlined above?
2. What other types of portfolio approaches might be useful to help an organization understand its technology investments and their impact?
3. Use a real life example to illustrate how portfolio management has or would have made a difference in decision making about IT investments.

9

Sourcing IT Services

The last consideration of this section is sourcing. The concept of sourcing was already introduced in Chap. 6, as it is a key focus of governance. In this chapter, we will delve more deeply into various aspects of sourcing with a focus on how sourcing affects the business value sought from investments in information technology (IT).

Sourcing of technology systems and services has been and continues to be one of the most hotly debated topics in IT management. An enduring challenge faced by organizational executives is deciding how much to do in-house and what to provision through external service providers. Outsourcing to external service providers is a popular way for businesses to produce and deliver products and services to their customers. Outsourcing of IT services is no different. Much of the IT-based services delivered by organizations have been outsourced to providers locally and offshore. In fact, companies such as EDS, IBM Global Services, Accenture, CGI, Infosys, Wipro, and others exist and thrive because of outsourcing. Outsourcing has worked well for some organizations but has been problematic for others. It is not the panacea that many executives hoped it would be. As with any other productive arrangement, outsourcing success depends largely on the characteristics of the contracting organizations and the context in which these arrangements are made.

Sourcing is not simply a choice between outsourcing and internal provisioning. It is about deciding among a variety of options as to how an organization will make its investments, both business and IT. IT investments cannot be treated as separate from other business investments. They must be considered part of the overall mix of investment options faced by organizations. Though many IT sourcing decisions are made based on the capacity and performance of the internal IT group, organizations need to adopt a more strategic stance that looks beyond the dichotomy of the internal IT versus outsourcing provider. They need to realize that the choice of sourcing options should emerge from a thorough understanding of the strategic intent of the organization as well as a robust assessment of its capacity to mobilize the resources to deliver on that objective both in the short and long term. All options are not equally available and can vary based on the characteristics of the organization, the context in which it operates, and the legacy investments already in place. Legacy investments, such as an enterprise resource planning (ERP) system, can enhance or constrain the choices open to organizations and create significant opportunities or barriers for innovation with IT.

Even though return on investment (ROI) is a key measure of investment performance, sourcing decisions cannot totally or only be based on this. ROI provides measures of efficiency in the use of resources, which is crucial in any decision making about investment. However, sourcing decisions also need to take the formal and informal relationships between client and provider into consideration. Good formal relationships, ensured and enabled by well-developed contracts and service-level agreements, are central to sourcing success, whether achieved internally or externally. Since contracts and service agreements are necessarily incomplete in their conception and development, it is the good informal relations that will be key to covering the gaps that might develop in the service delivery relationships. Some gaps can only be bridged through the goodwill that exists between client and service provider.

Sourcing Options

McKean and Smith[1] suggest that in making sourcing choices, organizations must decide on what services to provide internally versus what to provide externally and how to provide these services. Figure 9.1 outlines a portfolio of sourcing options. The X axis represents the options from internal to market (or external) sourcing. The Y axis represents the objectives from efficiency (make what we do better) at the bottom to strategic impact (change what we do) at the top. Each quadrant represents a general category of decisions. In reality, many overlaps may exist between the categories. However, the categorizations allow us to frame the portfolio of decisions that are likely to be taken by organizational executives.

---

[1] McKean, J. and Smith, H. (2003) Making IT Happen: Critical issues in IT Management, Chichester, John Wiliey & Sons.

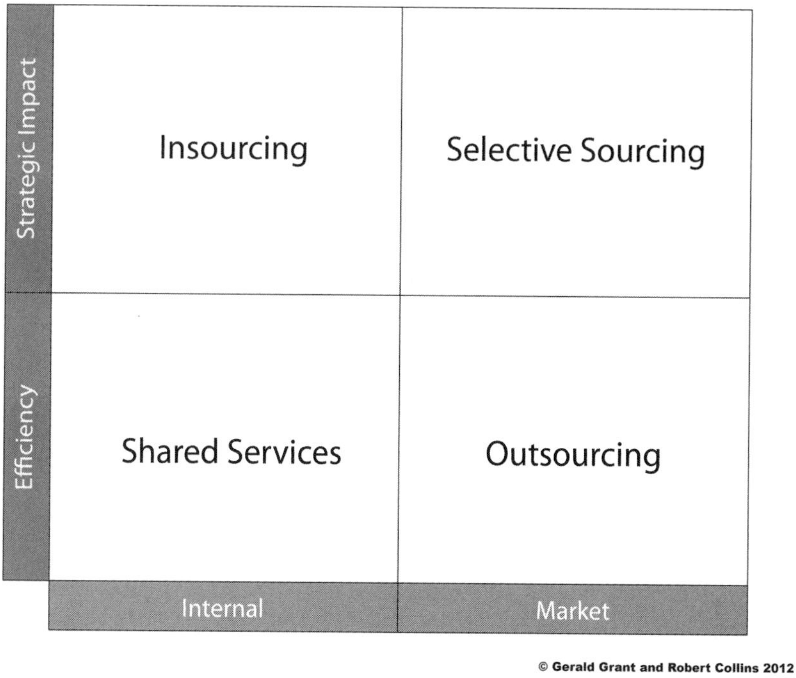

Fig. 9.1 Sourcing options

As the figure illustrates, for strategic impact, outsourcing is not the preferred option. To create transformational change, it is vital to be close to the business and have a weather eye for change, allowing for nimble and entrepreneurial responses to issues and opportunities. This is virtually impossible when outsourcing because of the dynamics of the contractual relationship between the supplier and the organization. In most outsourcing situations, the work to be done must be defined in advance with clear pricing assigned. Making significant adjustments midstream is difficult and may mean having to renegotiate or terminate the contracts originally agreed to.[2] Insourcing is far more preferable for strategic efforts. It allows for a tight relationship between business and technical resources. It provides the freedom to adapt and, in the worst-case scenario, allows management to cancel a project that is determined to be failing. Canceling a contract with an outsourced supplier can often be highly expensive.

---

[2] Lacity, M. C. and Willcocks, L. P. (2001) Global Information Technology Outsourcing: In search of business advantage, Chichester, John Wiley and Sons, p. 12.

This framework can also apply for systems maintenance as well as their development. Where a system supports a process that is the organization's differentiator (i.e., separates them from the competition), having that supported by in-house staff ready to react and change on a moment's notice may be vital. While attempts have been made to make rapid change and innovation possible in outsourcing arrangements, they have proven largely difficult to carry out in practice.

There is room for the market to play a role in strategic change. Often, radical change requires expertise that is not in the organization. Think of a switch from retail stores to Web sales and social media. It will be more expensive, time-consuming, and error-prone to develop or hire the skills in-house than it would be to purchase the skills. But this is not full outsourcing. The responsibility for the project remains with the organization itself, and the selective sourcing of skills and services supplements the internal team. Another good example of this is when an organization implements an ERP system for the first time. Bringing in process and technology expertise greatly increases the chance of success.

Selective sourcing can also be applied to software purchasing. Choosing the right prepackaged software can provide functionality much faster than developing the software in-house. This is especially true where an organization is extending from an existing portfolio. For example, a company with an ERP system that needs better information to make decisions might be able to quickly reach that goal by purchasing software that was designed to work with that ERP system, possibly from the same vendor.

Where efficiency is the goal, outsourcing becomes a more attractive option. For systems that are relatively stable, it can often be cheaper to contract out the support work to a supplier who has a lower-cost model than the organization itself. For example, suppliers who support the deployment and maintenance of PCs at an organization can use the same staff to supply a number of customers, cutting their employee costs. They can also develop better economies of scale with their suppliers (the hardware manufacturers), again cutting costs. PCs, being a commodity these days, are rarely of strategic importance to organizations. They have become more like office furniture. Outsourcing this work is common. This can apply to application systems as well. Many companies outsource their payroll effort to suppliers as this work, while important, is rarely strategic and generally highly commoditized.

Outsourcing can involve moving an entire system, or suite of technologies, and having a supplier provide them from their own premises with their own staff. No internal employees would work on any of it. The advent of cloud computing and software as a service (SaaS) offerings are making this an everyday reality. This is the most drastic form of outsourcing, which can have great returns in the short term but may limit future capabilities. It is also possible to outsource parts of a system or process. For example, a central bank announces interest rates every month. On the morning that announcement is made, there is a need to have a website that can support millions of hits within an hour before the markets open. For the rest of the month, there is no need for such capability. It would be foolish for the bank to develop the capability to handle that load in-house and have it sit idle 99% of the time. Instead, the Web hosting of that information can be outsourced to a supplier who can provide it cheaply because they can use the 99% idle time to meet the needs of other customers. (Think of a farmer who rents a piece of equipment needed one day during planting rather than buy it and have to maintain it.)

Internally, efficiencies can be gained by providing shared services. For example, having multiple email or payroll systems within an organization makes little sense. Yet older and larger organizations (such as governments) find themselves in exactly this situation for historic reasons. Reducing the support for such technology by assigning it to a single group supporting multiple user communities will drastically reduce costs and should not affect service. In the same way, developing application software using Service Oriented Architecture (SOA) and such methodologies will enable the same benefits to be realized in the application tier that is more often seen at the hardware layer.

An organization should be considering all of these options when sourcing their various service and technology solutions. Using this or similar frameworks as a guide, executives can plot the existing systems on such a quadrant chart to assess the mix of service and technology delivery solutions. By doing this, they can create a very effective tool for managing the sourcing portfolio. This will free up scarce internal resources currently allocated to low-value work and reassigning them to accomplish more strategic objectives.

Sourcing Providers

When dealing with providers who will supply some, or all, of the systems supporting the business, it is important to develop the appropriate relationship, measure that service, and manage the outcome. The responsibility for the harvest still rests with the organization, even though some of the work has been contracted out or purchased.

Internal Providers

There can be multiple ways of sourcing services and technology systems within an organization. A specific department may source its technology from within the business unit itself. This may involve staff who are not "IT" people. This may be a good option when dealing with a piece of technology (specialized handheld devices) or an outsourced supplier (sales tracking and forecasting) that requires little or no integration with larger IT systems and processes (farm). These are specialized gardeners. This approach has been successfully used in municipalities. For example, drinking water and sewer systems are controlled by specialized technology that is deliberately kept off the corporate network. There is no economy of scale by having this deliberately disconnected service managed by Central IT. Instead, economies of scale can be found by having staff contribute both to the business and technical aspects of the department from which the service is delivered.

Within business units, there may be IT departments dedicated to that unit. These are usually smaller than centralized IT departments. They deal with issues specific to that business unit and have, or develop, expertise in the business as well as the technology. Such a group would be less likely to deal with infrastructure and more likely to deal with tactical applications. This is common for manufacturing systems specific to a plant.

A centralized or corporate IT group is prevalent in many organizations. It delivers IT systems and services to multiple business units or departments. This group's responsibilities and activities cover a wide range of services across the IT architecture. These range from customer-facing applications to core infrastructure services (data management, storage, networks, and physical facilities). Centralized IT groups are able to deliver common services across the organization much more cost-effectively.

External Providers

External suppliers also come in different variations with different benefits. Any one or more of these may contribute to an organization's success. Some work with internal providers where others are replacements for organizational capacity.

One type of provider is the consulting firm. They provide staff to augment the IT or line-of-business departments. Such staff may be brought in because they have expertise that is not available in-house. Others may be brought in merely to beef up the numbers during times of extra work. Almost all IT departments make use of external contractors.

Software and hardware suppliers are another source. Commercial off-the-shelf (COTS) software may range from the ERP system controlling all the money flow in an organization to a point solution used by a specific department for a specific job. Such suppliers offer an alternative to internally developed systems. They rarely meet exactly the needs of an organization but they provide functionality faster and, through maintenance contracts, keep software and hardware up to date, freeing internal staff from a large support workload.

Between in-house and COTS suppliers, there are firms that will provide specific custom-built systems. Instead of creating an internal team to develop an application, the work can be outsourced to a software or consulting company that will develop the system to meet the exact specifications of the customer. This is often done when expanding into new areas of technology.

Whether systems are COTS, developed in-house, or developed externally, there is a choice of where they are hosted. Infrastructure may exist in the organization's computer rooms, secured by internal staff and managed by company employees. They may be totally hosted by a supplier who frees internal staff from worrying about the underlying infrastructure. Or they may be a hybrid, with portions housed internally and others elsewhere, perhaps in the cloud. Such a solution can offer greater flexibility in return for different cost structures.

Wherever they are hosted, there is still a question of how they are managed. An application or technology may be supported directly by a supplier rather than internal staff (the PC example cited above). Such support could extend to applications where the supplier deals directly with the user department to support the application, which may be hosted in-house, at the supplier's facility, at a third facility, or in the cloud. In the same vein, a system existing outside the bounds of the organization may still be supported by staff in-house due to its critical nature. For example, large data warehouses may be housed by a service provider, but the data are managed by internal Database Administrators (DBAs).

Managing Suppliers (SLAs)

Service level agreements (SLAs) are a set of measures agreed upon between the user and the IT department as to what is to be delivered for a particular business process and its associated IT system(s). Drawing on the harvest, the SLAs should be stated in business terms as outcomes from the process (as per the Values Realization Cycle [VRC]). This guarantees alignment of IT with the business. Too often, they are measured using IT metrics such as database transactions, network throughput, or the like. This often leads to arguments between IT and the people it supports, which, in the end, may result in misalignment between what the business wants to accomplish and what IT delivers.

With sourcing beyond the internal IT department, SLAs are even more important (if that is possible). SLAs should be agreed upon in advance between the user community, IT, and the supplier. They should use metrics that make sense to the business. While lower-level IT metrics are useful for debugging problems, these are not the goals that the organization seeks to achieve. Consequently, the contracts should not be based on these. A supplier will use the SLA to determine the cost of the offering and set the price at which they offer the product or service. (For competitive procurement processes, SLAs should be specified in the Request for Proposal [RFP]). The IT department will use the SLAs to monitor the supplier's performance and address issues before they become problems. The SLAs should be the basis of regularly (monthly or quarterly) meetings.

There should be a mechanism in the contract to change the SLAs. As part of the contract, this is a significant change; but changes in the business process or in the surrounding infrastructure or environment will happen over time. A defined method for dealing with them should be documented in advance. This will smooth the process and keep the relationship positive.

Of course, to have SLAs, it is necessary to actually measure. Setting standards and then never being able to assess if they are being met is totally pointless, yet far too common. For existing systems, most organizations will have to make measurements of existing performance. It is important to do this before engaging in contract negotiations. For new systems, it is not uncommon for the supplier to suggest the SLAs. In this case, IT's job is to ensure that the user community understands and agree to the SLAs.

Benefits and Drawbacks of Different Sourcing Models

Insourcing

Benefits

An insourced project provides almost complete control. All the staff are responsible to the organization and can be given direction. If change occurs, there is no need for negotiating contract changes or involving lawyers. Responsibility can be fully defined and managed.

Insourcing provides better possibilities for communication between business groups and IT. As everyone works for the same organization, there is common ground to begin with. It is simpler to put the necessary people together to hammer out issues and resolve conflicts. There is a higher likelihood that people are geographically close to facilitate more face-to-face communication. We know from experience that there is no guarantee this will happen. But a focus on the harvest from all sides will enable an organization to exploit these opportunities. At its best, this allows collaboration that is not possible with an external provider governed by contracts.

Alignment with strategy is easier when all involved work for the organization and are apprised of that strategy. Decisions will be made with that strategy in mind, which would not necessarily be the case for an external supplier. This is especially important when you are dealing with strategic competitive issues that should not be made public (e.g., mergers and acquisitions).

When developing systems in-house, the knowledge and competencies built up in the creation of those systems is retained in-house. This expertise is available to maintain those systems, to apply in future systems, and to ensure integration with other systems in the organization.

Change management is more easily accomplished for insourced efforts. If it is determined that the direction needs to be adjusted, the project altered, or the functionality changed, such a decision can be made, communicated, and then acted upon. Conversely, if there are external suppliers, negotiations will be required and greater risk introduced.

Challenges

Doing things in-house takes the focus away from core competencies. If you are using staff and money to develop/support technologies that are largely commodities, then those staff and that money are not available to work on systems that have strategic value to the organization.

Insourcing may cost more. Depending upon the situation of an organization, internal staff often have higher costs. Not just salaries but accommodations, benefits, and career management must be considered. This is especially true where staff are needed with specific expertise but the workload for such expertise does not warrant full-time staff with other staff to back them up. Scarcity of staff with the right experience and expertise is a challenge faced by all IT departments. A lack of skilled staff can lead to system failure and/or user dissatisfaction.

Head counts and payroll limits affect all organizations. Even if the right staff are available in the market, it may not be possible to grow the IT department to the size needed to cover the wide variety of technologies that need to be supported.

Innovation, when everything is insourced, is limited to the capabilities and competencies of internal staff. This is especially problematic with new technologies. Developing the skills needed to exploit these increases time and cost. Also, it is possible that opportunities will be missed because internal staff are unaware of new or changed technologies. This can be offset with training, but that increases costs. Staff will tend to use the tools with which they are familiar. For example, ERP teams will want to use the ERP to solve all problems. (When all you have is a hammer, everything looks like a nail.)

Insourcing is the least likely to benefit from economies of scale. There is no question that it can, but it often does not due to a lack of focus. Unless you are specifically driving those efforts, insourcing will always tend to add to the workload, rather than reduce it. Also, staff are less likely to offer up ways of reducing effort when they perceive that their job may be at stake if that is done.

Outsourcing

Benefits

The primary reason for outsourcing is to save money, and there is every reason, if it is done correctly, to achieve this objective. Finding a partner who can do the same work cheaper can be a win/win situation. Equally important is saving time. Sourcing to get to a result faster can be a major contributor to an organization. This may be doing work in parallel with an outsourced developer or buying COTS to quickly implement rather than develop homegrown systems.

Outsourcing can reduce staffing challenges. Often organizations measure in two currencies—money and heads. It is not uncommon to find that a department has the money to do something but lacks the ability to hire staff to do it. Outsourcing offers an alternative. By trading money for heads, it becomes possible to do more.

Outsourcing offers a means to shift internal staff from old to new technologies. By taking older, more stable systems and outsourcing their support, internal staff can be moved to more strategic projects. This not only gets the focus on the strategic organizational goals but also contributes to staff retention.

Outsourcing can provide expertise that does not exist in-house. Done right, it can get expertise cheaper than hiring full time employees would allow.

Service can be improved by outsourcing support and maintenance. Taking work that is done by staff as a secondary function, distracting them from other work they would rather do, and giving that work to a vendor dedicated to make it successful, will be noticed by the user community.

IT workloads expand and contract. But expanding and contracting the in-house full time staff to accommodate the variation in workload requirements is not realistic. Hiring contractors and outsourcing components is a common and effective means to deal with a variable workload.

Stable systems make excellent candidates to outsource (i.e., no need for cultivation or nurturing). It is straightforward to measure when change is limited. The future is relatively predictable, making it easier to draw up a solid contract. Such systems also are of limited interest to internal staff who do not see career advancement in being assigned to such technologies. Such systems, with clear outcomes, offer the best candidates for economies of scale.

Developing strong partnerships can provide a long-term benefit. Creating a strong relationship with a supplier can lead both sides to look for further opportunities to do business together. The supplier will get to know how the customer works and can make suggestions for improvements and identify further opportunities. The customer can draw on the supplier as a source of expertise and information. Where this is an ongoing relationship with a steady revenue stream, the supplier is encouraged to participate in discussions and investigations without putting immediate cash on the line in hopes of future revenue. These long-term partnerships can greatly expand IT's ability to create value for the organization.

Challenges

Treating IT as a cost solely to be reduced through efforts such as outsourcing is tempting but dangerous. Doing so may meet short-term goals. However, eliminating the internal expertise to innovate and apply technology to meet organizational strategic goals is a serious deficiency. Companies that did such drastic outsourcing in the 1990s found they had to rebuild their IT capabilities in the following decade, wiping out the expected benefits and setting them back over time. If you sell the farm, you can't plant anything new.

It is difficult to create a contract with a supplier that covers all eventualities. Whereas internal IT departments can be directed to change their approach, external suppliers require contract amendments, which involves lawyers and money.

Poor measurement is a common failure in outsourcing. Although it is never a good idea, measurement is often lacking for internally supported systems. When such systems are outsourced, therefore, there is no basis from which to develop metrics to manage the contract. A lack of clear metrics is a sure ticket to aggravation down the road. You cannot manage the contract if you cannot measure the impact of the supplier.

Outsourcing does not mean that you no longer need to manage. A lack of active management is a common flaw in outsourcing. Even though you are putting the system in the hands of a supplier, you still require staff to manage that supplier. The skills to do so are not the same as internal management. Managing outsourcing is more about contracts and metrics and not so much about managing staff. If problems arise without appropriate management, they will only be dealt with once they have become crises. Having a manager that can help avert crises is a cost that must be considered when outsourcing.

Depending upon the level of outsourcing, integration can become a challenge. If you lack access to outsourced systems or the expertise to work with such systems, it becomes difficult to understand the needs of coordinating new systems with these outsourced technologies. The supplier is going to have to add costs to provide that expertise and do any work needed for integration.

Poor contracts and SLAs will create disconnects between the goals of the supplier and the goals of the customer. The contract puts the power in the hands of the supplier. Any changes will usually involve more money, calling into question the value anticipated in the original outsourcing decision. While contracts can be terminated, the cost can be very high both in time and in the effect that such a change would entail. Also, most contracts have penalty clauses for early termination. Proving noncompliance can be very difficult and expensive, especially where the contracts do not have clear, measurable SLAs.

Outsourcing systems that are subject to change will involve additional costs. Such systems are not good candidates for outsourcing, as the workload is both high and not fully predictable.

There must be a clear understanding of what benefits are expected from outsourcing. Just as any system should have a clearly defined harvest that becomes the focus of all involved creating alignment, so an outsourcing contract must have that clear business value that all understand. Too often, outsourcing is undertaken because it *seems* like a good idea.

It is essential to choose an outsourcer with the expertise and ability to achieve the objective. This is especially true when an outsourcer is selected to build a new system. Choosing a vendor with great expertise in financial systems with whom you have a strong relationship is good. But choosing such a vendor to build a real-time system with mobile devices could be folly.

As well, all the benefits identified with insourcing are potential challenges with outsourcing. Outsourcing will reduce your internal skills and expertise, complicate your communication with user communities, and make things less flexible in the face of change.

The Right Mix

Sourcing is another portfolio of IT to be managed. Like all portfolios, finding the right mix of tools, partners, and investments is the key to delivering maximum returns. Rarely, if ever, is one sourcing option right for all IT systems in an organization. It is vital for the IT department to drive the sourcing discussion or, as has happened in the past, it will end up having sourcing decisions imposed upon it.

The key to sourcing is the same equation that is central to understanding the benefits and costs of any system—ROI. Sourcing has a significant impact on the cost (investment) side. But, as can be seen above, it can also impact the returns. When presenting options for investing in a new system, or continuing management of an existing one, it is reasonable to put forward the ROI of various insourcing and outsourcing options. Doing this will ensure that decisions are made based on real, measurable values and not on the basis of ideology or frustration.

Outsource Your Troubles—An Example

A global software company was growing by leaps and bounds. All this success was producing natural growing pains. Processes, and the systems to support them, had developed organically when the organization was much smaller and managers could easily keep an eye on things. The rapid growth strained these processes. Leaders were unable to get the information they needed. Work was falling through the cracks. Clearly the systems were not good enough.

This problem was most evident in the services branch of the company. Each country had always managed its own services business, supplying consultants to customers to help them take advantage of the company's software. While all countries used the same software, an off-the-shelf package bought five years ago, each used it in its own way. This had not been a problem in the past.

That was no longer the case. Global customers wanted the software company to provide a global solution. They were not going to manage consulting in each of their national operations. The software company had to grow up.

This was exacerbated by an increase in products from the company. Not all countries had the expertise to support all the new software. This required experts in one country to be able to support business in another. Suddenly, the systems that had been managing fine were no longer up to the job.

The vice president of global services proposed to the executive management team that the company buy a new, modern customer relationship management (CRM) system. This system, he felt, would resolve all of their issues and give them all of the advantages of CRM to improve their business. The executive team endorsed this proposal.

IT was appalled! The CRM system that Services wanted to buy was from a completely different vendor than the ERP system that managed all the financial business of the company. The integration would be a nightmare. Also, IT knew that the company lacked the data and consistent practices to exploit such a technology. The chief information officer (CIO) could see that this was going to be an expensive project doomed to failure. The CIO was not on the executive team but his boss, the CFO, was. The CIO laid out the business issues to the CFO explaining the effort and cost involved. The CFO was convinced that the risk was far greater than he had originally understood and also greatly concerned by anything that threatened the smooth operation of the financial systems embodied in the existing ERP system. At the next executive team meeting, the CFO revisited the CRM decision and had it reversed.

This created a significant problem between the services division and IT. The VP of services produced a memo to all executives detailing the failures of the existing system and laying the blame on IT for the fact that Services would be unable to achieve its objectives due to these problems. Below the executive level, recriminations and finger pointing became the order of business between Services and IT.

The CIO was on the spot. While he knew it was wrong to purchase the CRM software that Services wanted, it was equally clear that the status quo was not a viable option. Something had to be done to address the problem that existed now. The poisonous atmosphere that had been created made it very difficult to get a proper understanding of the real problems.

Taking the memo from the Services VP as a guide, the CIO invited in an outside supplier who specialized in CRM systems but was not attached to any particular software package. He gave them the mandate to come up with a clear statement of the existing situation for all the processes and systems used by the services division in all countries. The CIO gave his staff clear direction to support this effort and supply whatever the consultants needed. He worked with the VP of Services to persuade him that this unbiased review would be the key to any plan to resolve the situation. The VP agreed and made his staff available to the consultants as well. This immediately had the effect of lowering the emotional temperature and returning to business as usual.

The contractor quickly established strong relationships with all parties. They made it clear that they had no preconceived conclusions and that they were here to bring an end to the debate and resolve the impasse. Having established themselves as not being on one side of the issue or another, they found that they were able to have the discussions needed to properly document the situation as it existed. This succeeded where attempts by IT to do the same thing had met with resistance due to the politics within the organization.

The consultant returned with a report that laid out the challenge with clear business relevance and no emotion. The report showed that the challenges lay in both the processes and the application. The application suffered from many issues including a lack of reliability, lack of integration with other systems, and poor usability. The report also showed that addressing these issues would not address the major business problems. These challenges had, at their root, the differences in business processes in the Services organization. No CRM system nor improvements in the existing system were going to address that. The business had to define a common process to meet the needs of a global organization.

The Services division started discussions on a common process. This quickly bogged down in disagreements over how each country did their jobs and which were best. It was clear that a common process was not going to be delivered in the short term. In the meantime, complaints about the system continued to flood in to IT. The team supporting it was running flat out but was clearly not able to keep up. Since there was a headcount freeze, there was no way to add staff by hiring. Moving staff from other work would simply rob Peter to pay Paul.

The CIO decided to build on the strength that had been created by the consulting firm. While IT had a poor reputation with the Services division, the consultants were regarded as professional experts. He approached the company and asked them to take over support of the whole system. Some key staff would transfer to the outsourced operation while others would be reassigned to different work. The CIO was comfortable with this as it was clear that this technology did not have a long-term future. Therefore, he wasn't losing any capabilities that would be needed in the future.

The consulting firm put forward a proposal, which the CIO took to the Services department leadership. It was promoted as a solution that would give them dedicated support of world-class experts who already knew their business. It would allow Services to work directly with the supplier with no interference from IT. IT would cover the costs. The vendor would set specific service-level targets agreed to by Services and these would be measured and assessed monthly. Services was quick to agree.

Where IT would have had a challenge putting in service levels that required Services to define their measures, the new supplier had little issue with this. They were not suspected of trying to dodge the blame as IT might have been and it was clear that such things were needed for a contract with an outside supplier. That such things were needed between IT and Services was equally true but was clouded by other issues. The effort to define the SLAs not only allowed a contract to be written with clear deliverables but also generated much positive discussion within Services about how the system was used.

The outsourcer quickly turned their hands to the technical issues they had documented in their report. They put together a plan to address them with a schedule that was agreed to by Services. This commitment to address problems ended the constant calls to the help desk. As issues were addressed, confidence was built up. Within a year, all issues had been satisfactorily resolved, and the supplier was working against the SLAs that were now in place.

Could IT not have done all this itself without outsourcing? Certainly. But the cost would have been far greater. IT did not have the ability to add staff where it did have the money to outsource. More importantly, IT did not have the relationship with the users to create a positive environment for change. It was much easier to create this new environment by introducing a new element. The outsourcer did not have the "baggage" that IT and Services carried. Also, the need to have clearly defined deliverables in the contract was well-understood for an outsourcer where it would not have been so pressing for an internal effort. This allowed the outsourcing firm to quickly cut to the chase and deal with the important issues. IT could not have achieved this same result within the same time.

Did IT not undermine itself by admitting that they needed someone else to do the job? While this was the initial impression that some came away with when the idea of outsourcing was first proposed, in the long run it had the opposite effect. The CIO was clearly able to demonstrate why outsourcing had been used in this case where the technology was not strategic and time to resolution was critical. IT was able to use the SLAs and their impact on Services to talk to other departments about having SLAs for their systems. In this case, outsourcing was not involved, but everyone had seen the dramatic change in Services and wanted the same benefits.

IT was also able to shift staff from a very frustrating assignment to other work. This improved the overall atmosphere in IT and morale improved. Applying what they had learned from this experience to other non-outsourced efforts also gave IT a means to address lingering problems and provide a basis for future planning.

The tactical decision to outsource an old and troublesome application had provided the catalyst to change the company's understanding of IT's role. This, in turn, allowed IT to play a more strategic role in the organization.

Discussion Questions

1. What is the current mix of sourcing options prevalent in your organization?
2. What is your assessment of the sourcing portfolio?
3. For what functions (relative to IT) should your organization consider alternate sourcing?
4. How would you go about doing this?
5. What would the expected outcomes be?
6. Upon what would the SLAs be based?

10

Measuring IT Value Delivery

Throughout this work, we have referenced the harvest based on the Agricultural Model we introduced in Chap. 4. By focusing on the harvest, we have explained how alignment is created and maintained. The harvest has a key role in governance, investment decision making, project management, organizational transformation, and renewal. Being able to clearly articulate the harvest is vital. This section (Chaps. 10 and 11) will focus on exactly that. We will discuss what, when, and where to measure in order to assess the harvest and how that is expressed in terms of return on investment (ROI).

What to Measure

Organizations often engage in measuring aspects of their business operations. Often they do this as a matter of course because it is required for regulatory reasons or because it has always been done that way. At a minimum, organizations measure business operations and spending. Public companies measure operating revenue and profit. Beyond these, there are a myriad of potential measures that may or may not be tracked as a regular feature of the organizational governance process. Even if tracked, the measures may or may not have anything to do with the main challenges facing the organization.

There is a tendency for organizations to measure too much. Often any information available is reported, usually out of context of organizational strategy. It is reported merely because it is there. Having such measures, which are not related to strategy or core business processes, can be dangerous as they often distract the organization from focusing on its priorities.

© The Editor(s) (if applicable) and The Author(s) 2016
G.G. Grant, R. Collins, *The Value Imperative*,
DOI 10.1057/978-1-137-59040-4_10

What Should Be Measured?

An organization must measure the things that define its strategic objectives. A business must measure profitability, for example. But this measure is usually too general to allow for managing specific business processes. Consequently, along with general outcome measures there must be measures associated with each process. Those measures must tie back to the wider objectives, such as profitability.

There should be a manageable number of measures. For example, while there may be 100 things that impact a transit system's service to a community, trying to keep all 100 in the heads of the managers and directors is not realistic. The focus must be on the few things that matter to key stakeholders. This means that if such parameters are changed they will impact the high-level results as understood by the transit users and taxpayers.

Causal Relationship

There must be a causal relationship between what is being measured and the objective sought. There is no point measuring something that cannot be related back to the goals of the organization. If an organization's goal is increased market share, then measuring interest on cash reserves is not a useful effort, unless it has some meaningful relationship with market share.

Measures should be meaningful to their intended audience. Providing profitability measures to the folks on the assembly line may not be very helpful. They may not have a means to directly influence that measure. Holding them accountable for this may make them feel more a victim of the measure than an owner of it. Breaking down the measure to something such as throughput, and only showing them the subset of the measure that they affect, gives them the ability to understand the measure in context of their jobs. In other words, there must be an understood direct relationship between the measurement and the person to whom it is being presented.

Monetary Measures

Must all metrics be monetary? There is a tendency for businesses to favor this approach because money is part of any organization whether it is public, private, nongovernmental organization (NGO), or volunteer. There should, almost always, be some monetary measures because there are, almost always, costs involved. But investments are not always expressed in monetary units. Investments may be as much about key people or production resources as much as financial, though each may have a financial element. For example, an organization with a specialized system to control production will have a limited number of people who can effectively work on that system. Measuring how the organization is using these scarce resources is as vital as how much money is being spent. Just as you can't spend a dollar twice, you can't spread these people beyond their availability.

The results or returns expected aren't always expressed in monetary terms. For a bank or other for-profit company, it is most likely that returns will be expressed in currency values. Governments and other public sector entities, however, undertake investments to achieve social results that are not measured monetarily. For example, a municipality may seek to improve ambulance response time. If a city counselor tells residents that their taxes will go up by $10, those residents are unlikely to be happy. But if they tell them that for that $10, an ambulance will arrive two minutes faster when they need it, those residents are likely to be happy to pay the additional cost. The harvest of faster response time has value even though it is not expressed in the same currency as the cost.

The value of the measure is not always objective—for example, the ambulance response time. It can often be a judgment call that has to be exercised by the leadership of the organization and approved by its constituents (taxpayers, investors, donors, etc.). But just because it is not expressed in monetary terms does not mean it is not measurable. Multiple approaches to nonfinancial measurement exist. If a value is expected, articulated, and measured, it will be obtained (or not) in a transparent manner. If no measure is defined, or taken, then this is not planning and managing—this is *hoping*.

Alternative Measures

Hard data consist of clearly defined, agreed-upon metrics, such as profitability or cost ratios, that are not subject to much debate. When measuring profits, currency values expressed in dollars, Euros, yen, and other currencies are good hard data recognized internationally and across all disciplines.

However, organizational goals may include things that do not have easily identifiable hard measures. One common example is customer (or citizen or user) satisfaction. How do you measure the satisfaction of any person receiving the good or service provided? How do you effectively distinguish between high and low satisfaction? In this case, a soft metric is more useful. Unlike hard metrics, which have clear denomination and acceptance, soft measures seek results that are subjective and open to interpretation. Yet they do so in a manner that allows them to be used to assess the impact of processes, systems, and operational changes.

Surveys

Surveys are often used to query customers about their level of satisfaction with products and services. To do so in casual, everyday language is not very helpful as there is no standard way to express or summarize satisfaction. Satisfaction is a multifaceted construct (Is "I like it" as good as "It's okay for me"?). Instead, a Likert-like behaviorally anchored or ordinal scale can be applied. On such a scale, customers could be asked to express their level of agreement with a certain statement or to rate their satisfaction on a scale of 1 to 10. There is now a metric to measure. It must always be remembered that this is not as concrete as a dollar or a centimeter.

The initial survey may produce a result that doesn't tell much. If customer satisfaction is 5.5 on average, is that good or bad? What is known is that, with a customer satisfaction rating of 5.5, the company is making a specific profit or other goal. With this baseline, change can now be assessed. If the organization deploys a Web service to allow people to purchase and get support online, and then assesses customer satisfaction, it can tell if it has improved from 5.5 (or possibly deteriorated). The company can then assess the effectiveness of the new system without waiting for the year's profit numbers to come in.

A more effective way to employ a survey is to do gap analysis. In this type of survey, customers are asked both how satisfied they are with the product or service and what priority that product or service (or aspect thereof) has for them. For a transit service, a survey may ask about timeliness and fare price. In the model above, people might identify that they rate timeliness as 6 and fare price as 4. This might lead the transit service to focus on price. However, a survey that asks about both satisfaction and importance may find that fare price satisfaction is 4 and its importance is 4.5 whereas timeliness is 6 and its importance is 9. The gap for fares does not offer much room for improvement, whereas the gap for timeliness is big and shows a serious shortfall in meeting customer expectations. Service improvements focused on buses being on time are a much richer field in which to plant new investments.

Proxy Measures

Some things are just very difficult, if not impossible, to measure. In such cases, it is often possible to find another aspect that is known to have a relationship to the objective to be measured. By measuring this related aspect, it can be assumed that insight is obtained into the key factor to be affected, though this may not be foolproof.

A good example of this is employee morale. It is almost impossible to measure this directly. This is not a good candidate for surveys because employees may feel that their answers may affect their careers and thus hesitate to be candid. For smaller groups of employees, the sample size may be too small to be a valid reflection of the opinion of employees. How then to measure something that is so important to any organization?

Organizations often draw a relationship between employee morale and absenteeism. The idea is that happy employees are less likely to take time off work for sick days and other issues. While it is not possible to be sure of a 1:1 relationship, we can reasonably assume that there is some relationship. Absenteeism is straightforward to measure. Therefore, if we invest in technology to make employees' jobs easier and then find that absenteeism is reduced, we may be able to conclude that the change has positively affected morale.

Sometimes it is necessary to use several proxy measures to surround an unmeasurable but important objective.

What Is Right for Us?

What is right for your organization to measure? Of course that depends on your organization and its goals. But never doubt that there are measures that can be found that will give appropriate insight for decision making.

Where to Measure

Figure 10.1, below, you will recall from Chap. 5 is the Value Realization Cycle (VRC). Measurement is necessary at all points in the cycle. Do not just measure during projects or at year-end. It is necessary to make the right measurements throughout each phase of the cycle.

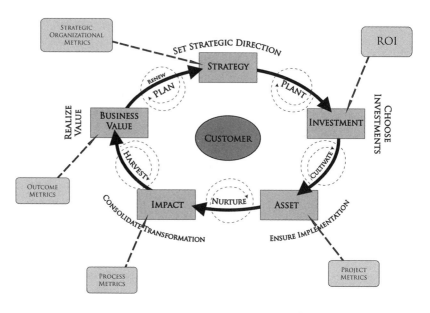

© Gerald Grant and Robert Collins 2012

Fig. 10.1 Where to measure

Strategy

At the strategic level, metrics must be tied to the strategic plan. These express the results expected from that plan. For example, if the strategy is focused on improving profitability, then profitability is a strategic metric. The strategy should express that as a measurable goal, and the measures can be taken to assess outcomes relative to that goal.

At the strategic level, it is the sum of all efforts toward the goal that need to be measured, not just a specific initiative. A company may, for example undertake several initiatives designed to achieve profitability—cutting costs, raising prices, adding product. Each of these will achieve some result that will be measured. But the strategic result is not necessarily the aggregate of the measures of those efforts. The correct result comes from the measure of overall profitability. One may find that the measures of combined efforts each contribute 3% to profitability, which means that it should aggregate to a total of 9%. But a calculation of gross sales minus gross cost may find that profitability has gone up by only 7%. This indicates that something else is happening beyond the accumulated impacts of the project outcomes. It shows that some other factor has had a negative 2% impact. If the analysis had looked just at project metrics, it would have missed this vital information.

Investment

The important measure for investments is return on investments (ROI). We will discuss the nature of ROI in the next chapter. Simply put, ROI combines how much an investment will cost and how much it will benefit. ROI is an expression of the harvest. When choosing where to invest, an organization will always have more potential initiatives in which it can invest than money and resources available to make those investments. There must be a way to decide among the possible investment options. ROI will provide a means to compare different investments options. Not only will it show which options produce the greatest results, but it can also show which results are best to achieve the strategic goals. This is done by choosing the returns that impact the measures articulated by the strategic plan.

For example, there may be three investments under consideration. One will improve profitability by 5% and cost $5,000,000. A second will improve profitability by 3% but cost $2,000,000. A third will improve return on equity by 4% and cost $4,000,000. If the strategic objective is profitability, then the third option can be eliminated. Options 1 and 2 can then be assessed based on available resources. If the organization has only $3,000,000 to invest, then it should choose option 2. While option 1 provides a better return, the investment needed to achieve that return is beyond its means at present.

Project

There are many wonderful measures defined for projects in methodological collections such as the *Project Management Book of Knowledge (PMBoK)*. These measures include things such as adherence to schedule and budget, user signoffs, code completion, and such. These project management metrics tell an organization the status of the planting and, as such, continue to be important to assess the health of a project even though they are not directly focused on the harvest. The metrics will tell an organization when it has deviated from intended objectives. At that time, the project should be assessed against its investment criteria to determine if changes needed will still produce an ROI commensurate with the original investment decision.

Impact

The result of the planting is an asset. The impact of the asset must be assessed by process metrics. This is likely to involve relatively detailed measures. For example, if the goal is to move business from a direct sales channel to the Internet, then tracking the number of transactions coming in through each channel and change over time would be most useful.

It is important that these measures be associated with business-related metrics, not just with the technology. The number of transactions in the database is unlikely to represent the number of sales transactions in the books. It is the latter that is having an impact on the business processes. The former (database transactions) may be a useful tool to debug the underlying technology, but it does not speak to the organizational goals.

Impact measures should have a direct relationship to strategic measures and to the ROI identified for the project or system. In our example, the number of Web transactions will show the same price but at a reduced cost than the number of direct sales transactions. This can be related back directly to a strategic goal of profitability.

Outcome

The outcome measures should be the same as the return identified in the investment. These are associated with the metrics that speak directly to the harvest expected. As noted above, measuring a change in the number of transactions (impact measure) is not the same as measuring the final result on profitability (outcome measure). If the strategic goal is profitability, then the outcome measure is the correct one to determine the success or failure of the project.

In our example, it may be found that, although the number of transactions coming through the Web channel meets the targets, the resulting profitability, when measured by actual sales minus costs for that channel, comes up short of the expected results. This might, for example, occur because of shipping errors commonly occurring in that channel that drive up costs. The impact measures show that the system implemented meets its target but the overall business process requires further work to meet the goal of ROI.

Relationship Among Measures

From the investment to the outcome, there should be a relationship that can be followed through the measures in the VRC. Bear in mind that, when we discuss returns, they are not always monetary. They can be expressed in any measure that represents value to the individual in the center of the Value Cycle (e.g., reduction in occurrence of diseases). However, they must still be measurable in order to ensure that the effort actually produced a result. The following provide examples of the relationship among the measures in the VRC.

A Cycle of Measures

- The return in the ROI should be directly related to a strategic measure
- The project measures should be kept within the context of the ROI identified in the investment
- The impact measure should assess the change brought about by the asset created in the project
- The outcome measure should be the same as the return identified in the investment and be the result of the impact brought about by the asset
- The opening strategic measure should change as a result of the outcomes of various investments and should be reassessed to determine what future investments are needed

Using the VRC to address issues of measurement provides the framework for cross-disciplinary assessment and discussion of organizational performance, including that of IT.

When to Measure

Time plays an important role in measurements. When to measure is a Goldilocks challenge. It should not be too early or too often or it will produce a cacophony of data that hides the real impact or situation. It should not be too late or, or otherwise, the time needed to assess and react will be missed. It needs to be done at just the right time so that it fits exactly within the business cycle that is being measured.

Business processes have their own timing. Sales transactions may happen within a short timeframe. But sales cycles may take weeks or even months, depending upon the product or service sold. When assessing the impact of multiple transactions, cycles may be quarterly or even annual. When trying to impact a specific sale, measurement must be in a normal business sales cycle. When trying to impact a quarterly result, measure quarterly.

Investments also have their own business cycle. It is common to measure too early by stopping when the asset has been created (after the planting). It is also common to measure only the cost OR only the return. It is the ROI that must be measured. The timeframe for that should be set when the investment decision is made. If the return is expected over several years, then the measures must happen over that full period and must cover investment cost and return for the entire time.

Organizations also have their own built-in cycles. Sales teams usually have a quarterly focus. Financial efforts are a combination of monthly, quarterly, and annual reporting, with an emphasis on the latter. Manufacturing has a cycle based on the time to change to a new product and the lifetime of that product. Each of the cycles should be understood when deciding when to measure. Presenting results within well-understood cycles is the most effective way to communicate impact and give focus to issues that may need to be addressed.

Whatever the cycle is, the same measures must be produced on the same schedule over the period of time identified by the strategy to which a particular measure is associated. Changing measures or timing can produce false information and result in poor decisions.

Strategy

Strategic measures are often measured annually. Rarely are they measured more often than quarterly. These are big-picture metrics summing up the results of work in all parts of the organization (e.g., profitability). Measuring too soon and too often can actually hide trends and waste people's time.

Investment

ROI should be measured regularly from the day the investment is decided upon until the day that the final expected return is realized. For example, if an investment of $1,000,000 is expected to take two years to implement and return $5,000,000 over five years then measurement starts the day the project is initiated and continues until the end of that five-year period.

ROI measures are most often done quarterly. This should be consistent with the governance process at the investment level. Monthly numbers will show too much churn, especially during the implementation phase, which may result in extra effort to explain variation that will naturally smooth out over a more reasonable timeframe.

It is also important to measure both return and investment from start to finish. Returns often come on slowly and start before the final project (planting) completion. Costs rarely end when the project delivery date is met. Ongoing costs for such things as support and maintenance must continue to be measured even after the project team has moved on to its next assignment.

Asset

Projects to deliver the asset, and their associated measures, should be reported to the project governance team monthly. Project managers will likely take weekly assessments.

Impact

Process measures can vary widely. In high-volume transactional systems, hourly measurements may be very meaningful. Longer processes may not yield telling results outside of a quarterly cycle. Process measures are associated with the minutest level of metrics and, as a result, there is a tendency for them to have the shortest period of all metrics in the cycle.

Outcome

This, again, will fit within a natural business cycle. If a process runs from start to completion within a single day, that may be the right period for measurement. If however, measurement is taken against a larger goal (e.g., cost reduction), a longer period than a single transaction cycle is more likely. Something as large as profitability is going to be difficult to discern for many organizations in less than a monthly, or even quarterly, cycle.

Tracking Over Time

No one measurement is particularly significant by itself. It is the ongoing impact of a system or a change to a system that we are interested in. This requires regular measurement on a recurring cycle that is also reported regularly. It is the trends, and the changes to those trends, articulated by regular reporting that tell the tale and get to the results identified by the strategic objectives.

What About IT's Measures?

Up to now, the focus has been on business measures. These are the metrics that define the harvest. But IT has traditionally tracked many measures that do not fit into the narrative thus far. These include things like various feeds and speeds for applications, databases, networks, and system availability. It is very common for these measures to be the core of reporting from IT departments.

Certainly they have no place in reporting to the business at large. It is this kind of reporting that has helped create the divide between IT and the rest of the organization. These technical measures, so valuable to IT, are generally meaningless to those outside the technology professions. When communicating to the business, IT must use the business language and the business measures. If those are communicated successfully, then there is rarely a need to introduce technical measures to the rest of the business.

IT, and the chief information officer (CIO) in particular, should be a leader in measures. Measures are a communication vehicle just as enterprise architecture (EA) and portfolios facilitate communication. This is a great opportunity for the CIO to show leadership to the organization at large and not just to the IT department. Using measures to communicate performance sets an example of how all parts of the organization can apply technology to facilitate communication and understanding in the business at large.

Using the right language and the right measures develops IT's credibility. Even bad news, communicated well, develops that credibility. Delivering the news using measures the business understands builds the relationship between IT and the user departments and takes emotion out of the discussion. Delivering the news with technical jargon only aggravates the users and leads them to conclude that IT does not "get it".

Do IT Measures Have No Place in Business Today?

All measures should exist within a hierarchy. The technical measures exist within this hierarchy, usually near the bottom. That does not mean they are unimportant. It only means that they are not useful for general communication. But when issues arise, starting a discussion from a business understanding and drilling down to a technical problem can be very effective. Then, when users understand how the technical issue relates to their business issue, the technical measure can be used to show progress and build up user confidence in IT. In the end, it is still necessary to go back to the business measures to show that a problem has been properly resolved.

A good example of this is the common measure of availability. Showing that a system is available 99% of the time is considered good. But the business department does not care about that. They only care about when it's not available. Having that 1% of downtime for a financial system occur at year-end is a disaster, no matter how good the 99% looks on IT's monthly report.

If You Can't Measure It, You Can't Manage It

Measurement is the key to understanding any business process and the technology underlying that process. It is the only way to understand the impact that any system, or change to a system, has on the organization and the strategic objectives of that organization.

Measurement is also central to decision making about investments. Understanding the return and the investment produces the ROI that allows different investment options to be compared. It points to the harvest that aligns the organization around the change to come. It allows the organization to assess the success of that investment and, when that success is not there, provides the rationale to change, or kill, any project or system.

Measurement of existing systems provides the basis for future investment. Problems, articulated as measures, show what is wrong. An investment proposal, in which the use of appropriate measures give clear indication of problem areas, provides the rationale for making corrective change and the urgency to assess the proposal against other investments options. Measures are the key for IT to justify investments in infrastructure. To do this, IT must be as good at delivering bad news as it is at delivering good news. By doing it with specific measures, it keeps the focus on business and builds the credibility IT needs in order to make a real difference to any organization.

Discussion Questions

1. For a specific system with which you are familiar, what measures are used?
2. How do these measures compare to the business objectives and strategy of the organization?
3. What other measures might be better used?
4. How may you use measures to effectively communicate good or bad news about IT investment results in your organization?

11

ROI

In Chap. 10, we discussed where and when to measure the harvest of value arising from IT investments. In this chapter, we will be more specific on how to measure. We will focus on return on investment (ROI), which has proven an effective means of measurement in many organizations.

A Word About Accounting for Value

As well as ROI, there are other measures such as net present value (NPV), internal rate of return (IRR), or payback period. These can be more or less complex and, in our experience, not as widely practiced as ROI. They can be very effective for organizations that practice them diligently. Even our discussion of ROI will seem somewhat simplistic to accounting professionals. For example, ROI is most commonly expressed as a percentage. However, we have seen value in expressing the return and investment separately to provide a magnitude to the value that is not as easily understood where a percentage is presented as ROI.

Our goal in this chapter is to promote the practice of measurement in a way that can be applied to any investment, IT or otherwise, without complicating the discussion with multiple measures. We have deliberately kept things simple to focus on the crucial issues and to make the chapter more comprehensible to those of us who have limited experience in financial matters. Each organization will have its own practices, and the chief information officer (CIO) would be well-advised to work with the chief financial officer (CFO) to understand and establish those practices.

© The Editor(s) (if applicable) and The Author(s) 2016
G.G. Grant, R. Collins, *The Value Imperative*,
DOI 10.1057/978-1-137-59040-4_11

ROI is an essential tool of communication and is how we define the harvest. ROI is the link between strategy and investment. It is the metric used to compare different types of investments or different investment options. It defines the goals of projects. It is the test of the impact of new assets as well as the value of legacy systems. ROI is a vital tool of governance. But so few IT organizations make use of it. In part, this stems from a lack of understanding of how ROI can be used. To some extent, its lack of use can be due to fear as it provides a means for highlighting accountability. It should not be feared, however. It is IT's best friend—providing the basis for justifying investments and making the right decisions.

What Is ROI?

ROI is the harvest. The return is the expected result from some conscious investment, past, present, or future. As has been seen in Chap. 4, the harvest is the source of alignment in the organization and the basis for important decisions. It defines the business value to be created.

ROI is also a standard that provides the ability to compare different investment options. These may be similar investments, such as a choice of software products, or there may be widely varying options such as the choice between an online support system and new vehicles. The use of ROI brings the IT investments into the mainstream of any organization.

Making investment decisions based on ROI avoids the trap of spending on "cool" technologies for their own sake. When the results are what matters, the value of the technology is purely that of its impact on those results, and its commensurate cost. Clearly defining ROI allows the IT department to force a technology sales team to focus on the value to the organization and not its technological differentiators, which may or may not produce any value.

By using ROI to make choices, emotion and personal preference can be moderated from the decision-making process. If someone believes that a particular technology is best, they need to explain how that will positively impact ROI relative to other options. This can be discussed more rationally, even by those with less technical skill, and a logical conclusion reached.

Because ROI is a measure that can be used everywhere in the organization, it provides a means to compare investments that may initially appear to be "apples and oranges". Any organization has a limited capacity to invest across all of the functions that make up that organization. How does one decide if it is better to use those limited funds to implement a GPS tracking system in a fleet of vehicles or to invest in training for staff in the sales offices? Each of these needs some investment and expects a certain return on that investment. By comparng the ROIs of those two potential investments, these disparate options can be rationally and measurably assessed and an appropriate decision made.

ROI provides an organization with a way to choose between options to solve any particular problem. Should we replace, fix, or abandon an existing system? What options do we have for each? By expressing all in terms of ROI, an assessment can be made of the alternatives and communicated through the governance process to investment decision makers.

For example, it may cost $500,000 to make changes to an existing system to bring it up-to-date with a return of $100,000 over each of the next five years being accrued from the impact. However, a new system may cost $1,000,000 but offer higher value of $250,000 per year over each of the next five years. This would be more compelling if the extra $500,000 were available. However, an alternative might be to scrap the existing system and use spreadsheets, which would cost an extra $50,000 per year in human resources but return $65,000 per year in savings from IT expenses to keep the old system running. The ROI here is still positive and the investment much smaller, freeing resources to be invested elsewhere. Which would you choose?

ROI Allows for Measurement

In any investment proposal, there should be an established ROI—the expected results for an expected investment. This now gives a metric to measure this investment. This measurement is not limited to the project to create the asset. It will continue throughout the life cycle of that asset.

During the project phase (planting), the focus is primarily on investment. Is the creation of the asset costing what it was expected to cost? If not, what steps should be taken to address this problem? If more time is needed, or less functionality is an option, what is the impact on ROI? Be sure to measure the impact both on the investment—how much more will it cost—and on the return—how it will change the expected result. With this in mind, the new ROI can be assessed against the original decision to invest. If the investment no longer makes sense, an alternative must be found that does, or the project should be canceled.

Consider a project to replace the mailing of bills to customers with email. Instead of printing the bills on paper, they will be stored in PDF format on disk. Then, instead of stamping 10,000 envelopes, there will be 10,000 emails. The cost to do this is expected to be only $10,000—the amount needed to implement an electronic mailing program. The savings in postage of $5,000 per month means it will pay off handsomely and quickly. However, during implementation, it is discovered that the organization does not have the email addresses of many customers. Worse, it does not have a standard place to store such information. To correct this, there will have to be a change to the database model and the enterprise resource planning (ERP) system. That will cost over $500,000. An alternative would be only to email those who have provided an address and to continue to use postal services for the rest. The first alternative drastically changes the investment. The second significantly affects the return. Either way, the original expectations of the investment decision are no longer valid and ROI must be recalculated. The result should be referred to the project governance process to determine if the project is still worth doing.

This measurement also provides a means of focus. Everyone from the board of directors to the most junior person on the project team should know the ROI and understand how what they do affects that goal. This is the essence of alignment. Equally, it provides a means of communication across all levels of the organization, from the most to the least technical person.

ROI is not purely for new investments. It should also be used to measure the value of existing systems. This is the basis of much portfolio management. While it is common to have systems that never had ROI defined, it is still possible to define it for future reference. Costs should be straightforward to identify and accumulate. These can then be used to justify the need for the business unit to assess the value of the system. Such a measurement can reveal where investments are needed or adjustments are required. This process should take place during the renewal phase of the Value Realization Cycle (VRC).

ROI and the Weather Eye

We have discussed how ROI can be used to assess change in a project that is not performing as expected. This is an example of change management using ROI as a measure. However, change does not always come from within a project. A project team may be on schedule to produce the asset expected for the cost expected, and the user community may be fully prepared to cultivate and nurture that asset to its maximum value. But the environment may undermine the original ROI decision. Market forces, economic issues, competitive actions, or even other internal projects may exert an unexpected force that will undermine all that good work.

Consider the example of competitive action. An organization has a project to provide online sales. Part of the ROI is based on the expectation that, being

irst to market with an online sales system, the business will capture market
.hare. However, a competitor gets there first, opening up their online store six
nonths before the new system will be ready. The portion of the return that
vould be gleaned from being first is lost. The ROI must be reviewed because
he return will now be smaller. Does it still justify the investment? Does it make
t even more vital because this unexpected action has introduced greater risk
o our business? An assessment of ROI, even though the project is on track, is
vital to answer these questions and determine how, or even if, to proceed.

Another change may come from the cost side. The vendor selected to provide the technology may be bought out by a competitor. The resulting reduction in the competitive nature of that market could allow that new supplier to
raise the cost of maintenance over the life of the asset. This change to cost will
affect the ROI. Again, through no fault of the project team, the situation has
changed and the ROI must be reassessed to ensure that the investment is still
viable and is the best use of limited resources.

The Components of ROI

Investment

Investment is ALL costs needed to achieve the return. Investment is NOT
just a subset of those costs. Too often, investment is viewed as just the capital
costs or the costs incurred by the core project team. It must include all costs
incurred. If any effort is necessary to make the return happen, then the cost,
including the time of the people involved, must be included in the investment
component of ROI.

It is not just the costs incurred by IT. There will be expenses within the
user departments both directly, and indirectly, affected by a new or existing
asset being applied to business processes. Training is a good example of such
costs. Training is part of the nurturing effort. By not including it in the initial
investment numbers, it makes it easy to cut from the budget late in the project. Such a reduction in nurturing threatens the realization of the harvest—
introducing risk in meeting the expected return.

Technical implications beyond the specific asset should be considered as
well. A good enterprise architecture (EA) will make it easy to assess integration requirements for any new, or failing, asset. If this integration is necessary to realize the return, even if it is carried out by a different team, its costs
should be included in investment. Similarly, if a new system requires changes

to another just to keep that one working to produce its expected return, those costs should be accounted for in the investment of this project.

Investment should also include opportunity cost. If, because the organization is committing limited resources to a specific investment, another investment using the same resources will be impossible, the potential return from that investment is an opportunity cost. That cost should be accounted for in the ROI for this investment.

Investment costs do not stop when the planting is done. The cost of nurturing and cultivation must be considered. Also, the cost of ongoing maintenance of the asset is needed. Many technology assets have ongoing support and maintenance payments and require a team to be available to react and support in case issues arise. These costs are part of the investment even though they are not part of the project to create the asset. This can be a huge cost that is often forgotten. A software technology with a 20% annual maintenance fee means that the cost of the software is double its purchase price for an asset that has a useful lifespan of 5 years.

The Return

The return, the harvest, is the expected benefit resulting from the investment. It is all the value created by the application of the asset to the business processes of the organization.

The return must be measurable. Many organizations express return in vague terms that cannot be assessed after the system is implemented. These may fit with broad organizational objectives. But if they are not measurable, then they are of no use for ROI.

A common, but misleading and dangerous, example is that of productivity. Many software products make claims that a broad number of users will each have a small productivity increase. When accumulated, they add up to what appears to be a large dollar figure that justifies a large investment. But after the system is deployed, the financial position of the organization do not reflect this improvement. Where did the productivity go? The problem with productivity claims is that they are often not attached to any budget. If no one's budget changes because of the expected result, the expected productivity will be eaten up by a myriad of other little tasks. There will be no reduction on the salary line and there will be no measurable amount produced that is greater than before. This is especially true where each individual will get only a small productivity boost and the value is spread across hundreds or thousands of staff. Such productivity is an illusion. To measure productivity returns, it is necessary to identify exactly which budget line item will change and by how much.

The return must be measured. Just because it is measurable does not guarantee that it will be measured. Unless the implementation plan defines exactly how and when measurement will be taken and to whom it will be reported, there will be no way to assess the results of an investment. Not knowing the value actually returned means that it is impossible to assess the impact of an investment or, in later days, to assess the ongoing value of a legacy system.

Just as there must be measurement, there must be assessment of those measures. For this to happen, there must be a governance process that tracks measures such as ROI and assesses systems, perhaps as a portfolio, over time. Governance of an asset is vital during its development but also through the life of the system. Only then will the full ROI be actually measured in keeping with the original investment decision.

The Temporal Aspect of ROI

Technology investments rarely achieve their returns in a single fiscal year. Significant investments made to bring about transformational change quite often take three to five years just to implement. The full realization of value usually takes years after that implementation is complete. Therefore, to assess ROI, it must be done over the full period of time from the moment the project starts until the day the system is taken out of service.

Since all technologies have an expected life span, the timeframe for the returns should not exceed the expected life span of the technology deployed. Having an asset that takes ten years to pay for itself but can be expected to be outdated and in need of replacement in five years is not likely to be a profitable investment. In IT, very few technologies are still valid (in their original form) five years after they have been implemented. Even if the technology is still viable, the change taking place around it is likely to call into question its continuing value. If in doubt, using a five-year life span is a reasonable rule-of-thumb for IT ROI.

A common mistake is to use different timeframes for return and for investment. This is most common when investment is only measured during the implementation phase and returns are only measured thereafter. The results of such proposals are false. The implication is that there are no costs after the planting. This is almost never true. Also, returns are often started before final implementation. Returns and investment measures should use exactly the same timeframe from start to finish.

Remember the orchard, where the asset bears a little fruit at the start, matures into a strong productive source and then, over time, sees regular reduction in returns until the asset is worn out. In the beginning, the asset needs more care to produce its returns. Over time, its production occurs as a matter of course. Later, more effort is required as the asset becomes less productive. All of this should be reflected in both investment and return measures.

Accounting for ROI

One of the biggest challenges to organizations is that investments are often made by one part of the organization while returns are realized by another. Nowhere is this more true than with IT. The effort to implement a new system is often paid for and run by the IT department. But the accruing benefits don't show up anywhere in the measures ascribed to IT. They are realized by other departments. This means that ROI cannot wholly be the responsibility of IT or of the user departments. It is a shared responsibility.

Consider a new system to reduce the costs of manufacturing. IT is charged with the responsibility of implementing this system. Some money is put in from an investment fund and other funding is found from within IT's annual capital budget. IT works with Manufacturing to produce and implement the system successfully. The final cost may be $2,500,000, the bulk of which is spent from IT's budget. Over the next five years, the system runs and accrues maintenance and support costs of $500,000 per year. This again, comes from IT's budget. The total investment over that time is $5,000,000. The resulting system allows Manufacturing to cut production costs by $1,300,000 per year. Over the five years that it is in production, Manufacturing saves $6,500,000. Most of the investment costs are borne by IT. Most of the return value is received by Manufacturing.

To put forward a proposal for such an ROI, it is necessary to involve both these departments. Realizing ROI cannot be done by any one of them without the other. Without the concerted effort of both Manufacturing and IT, little or no return would be realized on any investment. No investment should be approved that does not have these two departments coming forward together to achieve the result.

Such issues are even more challenging when the investment is made in infrastructure. When IT spends hundreds of thousands of dollars to upgrade the network, who receives the benefits? IT will receive some if ongoing support is reduced. But every department will see some benefit from this investment. That return will only be justifiable if other parts of the organization understand what the new network will do for them and see value in what it delivers. Just as with the manufacturing example, the investment should not be made just on IT's initiative. Those accruing the return must be on board to realize its real value.

It should be recognized that only very rarely does all the investment come from IT. Even if the project is funded and staffed from IT, there will be investments needed in the user departments. Changes to processes, training, measurement, staffing, and management all require the user department to invest above and beyond the creation of the asset. This is the nurturing phase of the Agricultural Model. If IT is seen as solely responsible for investment, these aspects are often missed and represent a real threat to realization of the return.

Given this, who should be accountable for ROI? If the returns are not realized by IT, how can IT be held accountable for those returns? Where user departments lack the skills to implement the system and handle its incumbent costs, IT bears the burden for accounting for the returns. Clearly, it is necessary for cooperation between departments. The focus on the harvest will give these various groups common ground for such cooperation.

In the end, only the department accruing the returns can be held accountable for the ROI. As owners of the business process involved, they cannot abdicate their responsibility. The implication is that, as those responsible, the user department must have the ultimate authority. IT must act as a service provider to that department making it possible for them to achieve the returns and make good on their responsibility. By using ROI as a primary measure, the relationships of departments is thrown into a stark light that clearly shows where authority and responsibility lie. While IT departments like to be seen as partners, they should be under no illusions as to the equality of such a partnership.

This should be reflected in any investment proposal. A proposal that does not recognize the user community responsibility for ROI and lacks investments above and beyond the core asset creation is unlikely to be successful. One that shows clear responsibility and leadership from the users, with a strong commitment from IT to make them successful, is the likeliest to achieve strong results.

Expressing ROI—An Example

The implementation of a new ERP system is expected to drastically cut costs for a number of departments, leading to significant savings. The cost of the software is $2,000,000 and the cost of implementation expected to be about the same. It is expected that savings will be $3,000,000 per year. The time to implement the project is expected to be two years. The initial business case therefore stated that the investment needed was $4,000,000 and that the return would be $9,000,000 in the first three years. This was quickly approved.

The only problem is that it isn't true. The implication here is that, at the end of three years the organization will have spent $4,000,000 but reduced costs by $9,000,000 to show a net gain of $5,000,000 in that time. But that won't happen. At the end of three years, the organization will find that it is still out of pocket over $2,000,000. Why?

First, the costs considered are only those of the planting. There will also be costs for the cultivation and nurturing phases. Changes to business processes and user education must be considered. These will amount to $1,500,000 including the cost to backfill staff assigned to the project. This money would have come from the departmental budgets and, not having been considered properly in the ROI, may not have been spent at all, putting the success of the project at great risk. Also, the software continues to cost money even after implementation due to maintenance and support costs. This amounts to $250,000 per year.

Second, the timing of the original business case is misleading. While it is true that the benefits will amount to $3,000,000 per year, what is not stated is that these benefits will not be realized in full until two years after the project begins. The third year of benefits will actually occur in the fifth year after project initiation.

A proper, though simple, view of the ROI would include all of this information and appear as follows (Table 11.1).

The return on an investment of $6,500,000 is $9,250,000. That is a positive return of $2,750,000 over five years. In simple terms, the ROI can be

Table 11.1. ROI example

$K	Year 1	Year 2	Year3	Year 4	Year 5	Total
Investment	3500	1500	1000	250	250	6500
Return	0	250	3000	3000	3000	9250
Annual Total	−3500	−1250	2000	2750	2750	2750
Cumulative Total	−3500	−4750	−2750	0	2750	2750

expressed as 42.3% over five years. This is still a compelling business case. However, if the executives were expecting $5,000,000 in three years, this number is not going to look so good. Expressing ROI accurately and fully is setting a project up for success. Expressing it inaccurately can take a successful project and make it look like a failure.

The ROI of Doing Nothing

Any investment decision should consider all alternatives in order to achieve the desired result. A common, and dangerous, mistake is failure to consider the impact of carrying on with the status quo. This "cost of doing nothing" is often assumed to be zero. That is rarely true. There is an ROI to status quo. There are ongoing support and maintenance costs. There are measurable returns that may or may not be achieving objectives and may or may not have a positive trend. Any consideration of an IT portfolio should put forward the ROI of doing nothing different. It is against this baseline that the ROI of potential investments should be compared.

Above and beyond the ongoing cost and returns of any system, there is also the opportunity cost of not investing. A proposal to invest will, at the minimum, highlight that opportunity cost to the governance bodies. Even if the decision is made not to invest, that decision has explicitly endorsed the opportunity cost of carrying on as is.

This is very important with regard to infrastructure. Regular renewal of networks, servers, and so forth, is necessary to keep existing systems functioning and provide a basis for new systems. If this investment is not made, a debt is being built up. The impact of that debt will be realized in reduced system reliability and performance. It will also be seen in limitations on future investment as the platform is not able to support such initiatives. Highlighting this cost of doing nothing to the governance entities is vital for IT departments. This is most effective when it is shown in terms of ROI reduction over time. This may best be seen in reduced ROI for various applications due to stress on their infrastructure.

The ROI of doing nothing should be an annual assessment as part of the renewal phase of the VRC. It should also be an alternative presented in any investment proposal to set the baseline against which the proposal should be assessed.

Consider the example of an existing application that has been running for some years. The application was written more than a decade ago using a software technology that has long since become unsupported since the original vendor has gone out of business. However, the application is still functioning and there appears to be no compelling reason to replace it. Common wisdom puts the cost of the system at zero since the organization is no longer paying maintenance on the software. A proper investigation would reveal that this is unlikely to be true. The system does not exist in a vacuum. Two years ago, an upgrade to the desktop operating system produced a large number of failures. Consultants had to be hired to make changes to the application to make it compatible with the new environment. This cost $250,000. Last year, the ERP system that produces the data consumed by the old application was upgraded. The data format changed and the old application had to be changed accordingly. At that time, it was found that consultants familiar with the technology were few and far between. A supplier from out of town was required who was not only expensive but also incurred travel and living costs, which increased the price. That cost $500,000. Because of these costs, this year, it was decided that an enhancement to the application that was desired by the users could not be undertaken. The users had hoped that this change would reduce their workload and commensurate costs by $100,000 per year. Above and beyond normal support, this system has incurred costs, including opportunity costs, of $850,000 over three years. That is the "cost of doing nothing." Similar costs can be expected in the future. If the cost to replace the system with a more modern, Web-based, off-the-shelf technology was $500,000 over the next three years, including maintenance, then the cost of doing nothing is actually higher than the replacement cost.

Risk

Risk is the potential that something will occur in the future to threaten ROI. Risk should not be confused with management. The idea that a project may be late is not risk but rather a function of a project that should be managed effectively. Risk comes from factors outside the immediate project or system control. Risk may be a threat such as natural disaster or cybercrime, or it may be external change such as market and economic conditions. Being aware of risk and keeping a weather eye for it is vital.

Sometimes risk is ignored when making investment decisions. This is consequential as it robs the organization of the ability to prepare. This represents a lack of both management and governance. Other times, risk is so feared that it is blown out of proportion. This can paralyze an organization that is too risk-averse. If no risk is taken, no improvement can be expected.

Risk is part of the uncertainty. Larger rewards warrant a larger risk. Showing a full understanding of that risk and how to mitigate it makes it easier for the senior levels of governance to approve a proposal by showing that balance between risk and rewards. Lack of recognition of the risk undermines the credibility of the proposal. Where tolerance of risk is appropriately low, large risk is unacceptable.

To manage risk, it is necessary to understand it. This can best be done by articulating the risk's potential impact on ROI. It is important to remember that risk does not guarantee there will be an impact on ROI. The impact will only be true if the risk cited actually occurs. The cost of a long power outage to a computer room has a potentially large impact on a wide variety of systems. But that is only true if that outage actually occurs.

How then do you justify investment to reduce risk such as disaster recovery, business continuity, and security? There are no returns in the traditional sense because, if life is good, any investment will not pay off. Only if there is trouble will there be a direct ROI.

In such cases, an insurance model should be employed. We insure things in case something happens. We pay some amount that is guaranteed to be spent in order to avoid some greater amount that may have to be spent. This requires both an understanding of the cost of some potential risk as well as the likelihood of such a risk. Different organizations will use different formulae to assess risk, and IT should work with Finance and the governance structure to agree upon a means to express risk. Regardless of whether an organization has such formulae, IT should be putting forward the facts for consideration by the governance structure.

Once an organization has established the cost and likelihood of risk, there is a baseline against which to assess investments to mitigate risk. Such investments should, obviously, never cost more than the cost of the risk itself. You wouldn't pay $1,000,000 to insure a $500,000 building. Neither should an organization invest in expensive mirroring sites for applications that the organization can live without for long periods of time (e.g., could paper be used while the ERP system was unavailable for a week?).

ROI Is Not Certainty

Returns and costs are rarely guaranteed. It is therefore, inappropriate and foolish to pretend that they are. An investment proposal that presents ROI as if it is certain lacks credibility and is likely to make trouble for those responsible for the investment down the road. The Agricultural Model tells us to have a "weather eye" because change will occur. This is as important in our investment proposals as it is in our asset management. Showing that the possibility of change was considered and still recommending the proposal enhances the credibility of the proposal and the IT department behind it.

When offering ROI, be prepared to offer a range of ROI to reflect the potential for change and risk. A proposal might contain a best-case ROI, a worst-case and likeliest outcome, or middle-ground ROI. By putting bounds on the ROI, the investors are getting a more accurate sense of the ROI they can expect. Presenting a guaranteed single number actually lacks credibility. A range of returns also can serve as an indicator of risk.

If we look back to the example of the online sales system contemplated earlier, ROI might be expressed as follows: The best case is where we are in the market with this technology for two years before our competitors. That would be an ROI that represented a $10,000,000 return on a $2,500,000 investment over five years. The worst case is where our competitor is in the market one year before us. (As they are not there now, and the project will take two years, it cannot be expected that they can do better than that.) In that case, the return would be only $4,000,000 on an investment of $2,500,000 over five years. Most likely, the competitors will respond within one year and the return will be $7,000,000 on an investment of $2,500,000 over five years.

Mandated Requirements

Often, investments are made because it has been mandated by some greater authority. This is not an excuse to avoid ROI. It is still necessary to communicate cost and expected results of any investment. Also, it is necessary to have a means to compare potential solutions, both technical and nontechnical, to any investment, regardless of any mandate.

Take the example of a municipal government. A state or provincial government might mandate that some program be implemented. The department responsible to implement it is likely to want a system to automate the process. They are likely to say that they don't need approval for the investment because it has been mandated. However, ROI calculations may show that such an investment is unwise. If the mandate states that there will be a penalty of $5,000 per year for noncompliance and the cost of a new system is $500,000, then it would take 100 years of paying penalties just to break even on the system. This is a bad investment regardless of any mandate. (And such a cost-benefit analysis can be used to push back on the mandate.)

ROI

The ROI is the harvest. It is the most important measure of any system whether it is an investment in a new system or an old legacy technology. No proposal can be properly assessed without an understanding of ROI (and the ROI of alternatives). It is not possible to assess the value of a portfolio of technologies without understanding their investment costs and returns. It is vital for the renewal phase. Finally, and most important, ROI is the key to having a business discussion about the technical systems, their value, and their priority to any organization.

Discussion Questions

1. Does your organization use ROI to assess potential investments?
2. If yes, outline how ROI was used to justify and/or assess a particular investment? What were the aspects of return and investment that were used?
3. If no, how might ROI have been used? What aspects of return and investment would be necessary?

12

The Role of Leadership

As the Value Realization Cycle (VRC) shows, it is the entire organization that is needed to get a return from investments in information technology (IT). IT plays a critical role in this, and the CIO must be an effective leader to bring about real value. However, the CIO cannot do it alone. In this chapter, we examine the roles of the various organization leaders in the VRC.

The Chief Information Officer (CIO)

The idea of a chief information officer (CIO) is a relatively new concept in organizations. There have been chief executive officers (CEO), chief operating officers (COO), and chief financial officers (CFO) for many decades. These roles are all understood to be among the most senior in any organization. They are roles that cross the boundaries of departments and divisions. They are not focused on the specifics of day-to-day business (or if they are, something has probably gone wrong). They are the guiding, or sometimes restraining, hands that operate across the entity, uniting it and ensuring that it is fulfilling its purpose in a manner consistent with its goals, with the law, and with the professional standards expected of that organization.

Do CIOs measure up to this standard? Are they leaders of the whole organization or are they more the senior representative of IT? Is their focus on the broad goals of the organization or do they spend their efforts dealing with the details of specific situations and projects? Are they focused on the business or are they focused on technology? For far too many organizations, while the

© The Editor(s) (if applicable) and The Author(s) 2016   **173**
G.G. Grant, R. Collins, *The Value Imperative*,
DOI 10.1057/978-1-137-59040-4_12

CIO title exists, the role is commonly seen as that of the head of IT, focused on technology and working at a level below that of the other CxO positions.

The Two Facets of the CIO Role

For most, if not all, CIOs, there are two roles that they must fill. There is the role as head of the IT department. This is a role that is focused inwardly, looking at IT. Then there is the role of organizational leader, standing apart from the IT department as the CFO stands apart from the finance department. This is a truly corporate role that is focused outwardly looking at the entire organization and the environment in which it exists. Let us focus on each of these two roles.

The Department Head

The department head is in very much the same position as any other vice president or director in the organization. They have a staff and a budget and are responsible for carrying out specific functions within the overall organization. They must represent their department and work to ensure that it is properly funded and staffed to do the job asked of it. They must be a leader to their department, someone upon whom the management and staff can rely for direction and communication.

As a department head, the CIO sets goals and direction for the IT department. What is the workload expected of the department? Are they in a position to cope with that workload? How is the effectiveness of the department measured on a financial, technical, and service basis? What should the targets be for those measures? How is IT performing against those targets? Understanding the goals of the overall organization, the CIO must ensure that IT is working in line with those goals and making a positive contribution.

The CIO is the leader of a significant number of employees. Is it the right number of people? Are they the right people? Are they in the right jobs? Do they have the right skills for technology, support, and management? Do people have career paths and are they progressing along those paths? With the IT management team, the CIO must bring groups of individuals together to operate as effective teams.

The CIO is a budget manager. How much money will be required to carry out the tasks demanded of the IT organization? How is it performing relative to the budget that was allotted to IT? Will it stay within budget? If there are unexpected challenges, how can the budget be adjusted to address them? IT is a significant expense for any organization, and this expense must be seen as being managed effectively.

CIOs are an important conduit of information. They must provide direction to their department by communicating the organization's goals and explaining how IT will work toward their goals. They need to keep their department informed as events progress to ensure that it has the information it needs to carry out its duties. They must also communicate outwardly from IT to the rest of the organization, explaining what is happening in IT and what can be expected from this department. They should not be doing all the communication just as they should not be doing all the people management, but they lead this effort and are ultimately responsible for it.

The CIO must worry about technology. Is the organization using the right technology? Is it being used the right way? Is the maximum benefit being achieved? At the least cost? What new technology is coming that may affect the organization in the near future either in a positive or negative manner? What old technology is part of the organization's legacy that may need attention in the near or distant future? Are the right policies in place for things like security and privacy, and are they being followed?

This is a very big job. It requires an individual who can operate at the most senior levels yet is sensitive to the nuances of the details. It requires someone who can understand the organization as a whole but who is also fluent in technology and understands its fast pace of change. They must be able to effectively communicate with every part of the organization. Such a workload can easily take up every available minute of every day. But if it does, then the individual is not acting as a chief corporate officer. Getting the IT leadership role right, makes the individual only a very good director (or VP) of IT.

The Corporate Leader

A CIO must go beyond just IT leadership to be part of the overall organizational leadership. An effective CIO is seen as a leader not only by the IT staff but by any staff anywhere in the organization. The CIO cannot be just a champion and defender of IT. They must be a champion and defender of the whole organization. This requires a very different mindset and viewpoint from that of the department head.

As a corporate leader, the CIO must be focused on the goals and challenges of the organization as a whole. What is it trying to achieve? How is it doing relative to those goals? Are these the right goals? How does it compare to others in the same space? At this level, the job has very little to do with technology. While, no doubt, CIOs will be influenced by their technological experience, they must not fall into the trap of reducing their contribution to that of a department head. The CIO must be a thought leader for the entire organization.

The CIO must be a communicator for the entire organization. As we have seen throughout this book, the focus on value requires a common understanding of what that value is and how it is achieved through the VRC by all facets of the organization. The CIO needs to be part of this communication process. Again, this is not about technology. It is about the organization's objectives and strategy. The CIO must be aware that the organization will never realize value from IT if it does not first have a proper understanding of value. No other leader in the organization besides the CEO has such a driving impetus to ensure that strategy, goals, and value are understood consistently and widely throughout the organization.

The CIO does have a technology mandate. While closely aligned with the technology mandate of the IT department of which they are the head, it is not the same mandate as that of their role as a corporate leader. As a corporate leader, the CIO must look at how technology can contribute to the goals and strategy of the organization. Where could technology be applied to meet those goals? What challenges are departments facing and how can technology contribute to meeting those challenges? Where is technology being used ineffectively or inappropriately and what can be done to correct that? How are competitors using technology? Customers? Suppliers? How are organizations that aren't related having success and what could be learned? This is more the blue-sky, out-of-the-box thinking that challenges convention and quite often challenges the IT department. This is not incremental but transformative thinking. Just as the CFO looks at how the organization uses money and considers various sources of funding, so the CIO must look at technology.

Also, just as the CFO is focused on financing, the CIO should be focused on information. Information is very much a currency, often more valuable than dollars or Euros. What information does the organization have? How does it use it? How does it share it? What information does it lack? Is there a common understanding of that information or does each department have a different view? Or, worse, do they each have different sources of information? Can the information be trusted? Note that the focus here is not on data. Data is how information is managed and that, while vital, is a secondary issue that is instantiated in databases and nonstructured sources. The focus here is on information, looking at it solely from the viewpoint of the business processes and its flow through the VRC.

The CIO must be a colleague to every department. Effective CIOs are seen as a source of solutions to be consulted by their peers. This is possible only when the CIO is seen as someone who understands that department's part of the business. If the CIO is seen as a technology leader only, this will not suffice. He or she must be a business leader and must be understood to have the skills and understanding needed to solve business problems.

Perhaps, more than anything else, the CIO must be a great communicator. He or she must be able to talk to any part of the organization in the language of that function. This does not necessarily mean speaking English, French, and Chinese (although that might help!). It means being able to speak about the production line to Manufacturing, deal making to Sales, and accounts receivable to Finance. It is also about being a translator. CIOs must be able to effectively translate the business needs into a technology context and vice versa. It should also mean that they can translate sales to manufacturing and finance to marketing. The other CxO executives are expected to do this. The CIO should be no different.

To be an organizational leader, CIOs must be able to remove themselves from the IT department. They must be able to operate across the entire organization. They have to be welcomed into each department and sought out when challenges arise anywhere in the organization. The ability to understand the strategic goals and situation and communicate them effectively to anyone from any part of that organization is essential. These are not the things one learns as one rises through the ranks of IT. But it is these things that sets CIOs apart from other department heads and warrants their having a CxO title.

The Path to Corporate Leadership

Few IT organizations are in a position for the CIO to suddenly step up from being the department head to being a corporate leader. This is true whether that leader is new to the organization or has been in the role for some time. Our observations and experience suggest that there is a path to elevate the role from one of departmental responsibility to one of organizational leadership.

The first focus of the CIO must be credibility. What is the view of IT within the broader organization? Is it a trusted partner or a necessary evil? Are systems up and reliable or is IT the butt of criticism? Is the focus on the future or on the backlog? It is not possible to stake a claim for organizational leadership when the email system is down yet again. Before any discussion of a broader role is broached, CIOs must focus on the IT department itself. They must establish their credibility with the rest of the organization. There is no magic to this. It is the hard work of ensuring that the organization is functioning effectively, that systems are up and running and that the communications channels are open and effective at all levels.

An assessment of IT's credibility cannot be obtained by looking at the IT department. It can only be ascertained by talking to other departments. When the CIO drops in on colleagues, what do they want to talk about? If it is how to solve their business problems, then credibility is good. If, and this is more likely, it is why there continue to be recurring issues, then the credibility is insufficient to build upon. While resolving any issues will involve getting lower levels of the IT department to work effectively with their counterparts in the user department, taking the temperature at the level of the department head will be the best assessment of credibility. In the Agricultural Model, this is the equivalent of walking through the fields and checking the crops. It is, in fact, the start of the renewal phase of the VRC.

Once IT has established a sufficient level of credibility, it will be possible to have a conversation with other departments about what they are doing instead of what IT is not doing. The next area of focus is to build the relationships at the executive level and on these topics. It is not uncommon for new CIOs to go to executives demanding to be at the strategic table only to find that their efforts are undermined by a lack of appreciation from their colleagues elsewhere. Before the CIO can stake a claim to organizational leadership, he or she must establish strong and trustworthy relationships with peers and between IT and user organizations that goes beyond day-to-day running of the systems.

Most vital to this is being able to speak in the language of the user department. This is very challenging for individuals who have risen through the ranks of IT and have a tendency to see the world through the technology. There needs to be common ground for this relationship. Fortunately, there is a Rosetta Stone that will serve the purpose—the Value Cycle. All departments need to be able to understand their role in the organization relative to the customer (client, citizen, stockholder, etc.). To be able to speak about the business of other department heads, it is necessary to understand how their department helps deliver value to the person at the center of the Value Cycle. Rather than talking about technology, ask about their work. Listen to them and communicate back what has been learned in their terminology. This will provide the basis for a relationship. Bringing technology to bear on their issues in their terms will then build that relationship. This will also allow the CIO to help the whole IT department understand the user community in business, rather than technological, terms. That will continue to build both the relationship and the credibility.

IT makes a lot of demands on user departments. They are expected to know what they want. They are expected to be consistent. They are expected to communicate. They are expected to tell the whole story. They are also expected to have some responsibility with regard to technology in areas such as security and asset management. As CIOs reach toward corporate leadership, they add additional expectations with regard to openness, strategy, measurement, and responsibility. All of these are necessary to ensure that an organization is going to get value from its investment in IT. But before they look to the users to meet these demands, they should first look at their own IT department. Does IT practice what it preaches? Is it open and forthcoming? Does it listen to the needs of others? Does it have measurable objectives that tie to strategy and are expressed in terms of the Value Cycle? Does it communicate those measures? Does it operate in a consistent and predictable fashion? Again, these issues go to credibility but they go beyond that. As corporate leaders, CIOs are going to want to recommend changes to the organization. Before doing so, they must make sure that their own house is in order. By doing so, they provide an example that shows real benefits that others can follow.

Technology Talk

But somebody has to speak to the technology! This is true. But must it be the CIO? Consider the CFO. A good CFO doesn't talk about debits and credits, forms, tax law, and accounts receivable. They talk in terms of organizational goals, albeit with a bent to the financial. Behind the CFO are important people like the treasurer, auditor, financial analysts, and accounts receivable clerks. When it is necessary to delve to the details, these people come to the fore. But for organizational leadership, the CFO speaks the language of the organization.

So it must be for the CIO. There must be a supporting cast who can, in the context of the CIO's organizational leadership, speak to the various technologies and issues that dominate the thinking of IT. By presenting an IT organization led by an individual conversant in business supported by technical expertise, the CIO is putting forward real organizational leadership. This means, of course, that there must be a strong management team within IT that can do that. That team may be supported by external suppliers and partners. Not only does this group speak to the technology, but it is the team that must free CIOs from the day-to-day responsibilities that would otherwise consume all their time as department heads thereby allowing them to play the role of organizational leader.

Finally, we have noticed a consistent factor that must be taken into account—time. Patience is perhaps the most vital asset when seeking to move from the CIO as department head to the CIO as organizational leader. This is rarely a journey that takes weeks. Far more likely, it is one that will take two or more years. Leadership is about the long term. The leader must have the patience to carry out a plan with an eye on the long term.

CIOs Need to Be Organizational Leaders

Fifty years ago, the idea of CIOs being organizational leaders would certainly not have been the case. Technology was in the back room. It supported back office practices. It affected specialists but was remote from most people in the organization. Rarely, if ever, did technology reach beyond the organization to influence customers, suppliers, citizens, shareholders, or donors. In that world, organizations needed a good department head. There was no need for a CIO.

How different the world is today! In the average organization, more technology walks in the door with employees, customers, and suppliers than the largest organizations had on their books even fifteen years ago. Virtually all employee use IT assets in some part of their job. Organizations that have not extended their infrastructure to embrace those outside the internal organizational chart are doomed to failure. Technology, even more than money, has become a ubiquitous part of everything every organization does. If a CFO is needed to guide the use of financial resources, then it is equally important that there be a CIO to guide the use of technology and the information that is gleaned through its use.

There is even more pressure on the CIO than the CFO. How money is used does not change every three years. But technology cycles do move that quickly. If no one in the organization is taking technology change and the potential of technology into account, then that organization is lacking a significant capability. This leaves it open to attack by more capable competitors or dooms it to obscurity by customers, citizens, and shareholders who simply expect better.

An effective CIO as an organizational leader who understands and speaks in terms of the business is as vital to an organization as a high-quality CFO.

The CIO's Role in the VRC

CIOs have a significant leadership role to play in the VRC. This starts with strategy. They need to be an influencer on organizational strategy—bringing the power of technology to bear on the challenges facing the organization. Communicating that strategy, both to the organization as a whole and especially to the IT department, is the primary role of the CIO.

Selecting the investments, or plantings, to be made is also a key area where the CIO must be involved. The choice of investments and the measures used to determine their value (the harvest) is something that the CIO needs to be specifically aware of and be able to clearly communicate. The CIO is a driver, ensuring that these factors are being used in the decisions to be made. Note that it is not necessarily the CIO's role to choose the investments being made but rather to influence the decisions made through the planning process involving the entire organization.

The CIO also needs to ensure that the organization is taking on a reasonable amount of work that can make the kind of difference that the organization needs. There can be too much work using more resources than the organization can reasonably apply (trying to plant more than the farm can support). There can also be too little work resulting in a harvest that will not get the organization to its strategic goals (leaving fields fallow). The CIO, as both an organizational leader and the head of IT, is in the best position to judge the overall effort being undertaken in light of the goals set and resources available.

The responsibility for the creation of IT assets, whether that is through purchase or through development within the organization, primarily rests with the IT department and is therefore the responsibility of the CIO. CIOs themselves are not the ones who should be guiding this process in detail. Rather, they must ensure that the governance process is in place around any project and that it is addressing the project at the appropriate level. This means that CIOs need to keep everyone's eyes on the prize — the harvest — and they need to be sure that a "weather eye" is being applied to look for change and challenges that must be addressed within the project and the governance structures.

This continues through the cultivation stage to ensure that the asset is adapted to the needs of the organization, bearing in mind the strategic goals that have been set. The CIO needs to continue to be involved at a senior level of governance, focusing on the harvest and ensuring the governance process is operating effectively.

In the nurturing phase, the leadership of the project normally shifts to the business units involved. This does not mean that the CIO drops out at this point but rather moves to more of a supporting role, working with the business leaders and ensuring that the IT department is operating effectively to support the nurturing process. This will ensure that the asset that has been developed will be employed effectively to deliver the impact that is required. Again the focus stays on the harvest and the governance process.

With the cultivated asset in place, nurtured so that it is producing an impact on the organization, the focus now shifts to obtaining the harvest — the business value that was sought when the investment decision was made. The CIO's role here is almost exclusively as part of the governance process. The harvest must be brought in and must be recognized as such. What was achieved? How does the resulting value compare to the expected value? Was any of the value appropriated away in unexpected ways? Why was there any variation from the initial plan?

In the renewal phase, the CIO should act as the facilitator and coordinator to ensure assessment of the impact on the strategy. Did the project or system meet the objectives that were expected? Did this resulting business value or harvest impact the organization as expected by the strategy? With this knowledge in place, does the strategy need to be changed to account for the new situation? In most cases, the answers to these questions will have to come from the rest of the organization. The CIO's role is to provide a framework within the governance structure. Therefore, when future investment decisions are made, they will reflect the new reality.

Ensuring that the organization moves effectively through the VRC is the responsibility of everyone within the organization. It is not reasonable to assign responsibility for this solely to the CIO. The CIO, as the leader in organizations who looks at the impact of technology, is in the best position to coordinate this effort and to ensure that it happens. The CIO normally does not have the authority to enforce such behavior but rather can identify where it is and is not happening and ensure that it is being addressed appropriately.

The CEO's Role in the VRC

The CEO has a primary role for strategic direction for the organization. In the VRC, the CEO is the leader at the start where strategy is the focus. While CEOs are not necessarily responsible for delivering all components of the strategy, they are responsible for ensuring that an effective and coherent strategy is in place for the organization. Furthermore, they are responsible for communicating that strategy to the entire organization. This creates a clear and consistent view of the goals that the strategy defines. In this role as communicator, the CEO is supported by the executive management team including the CIO.

Investment decisions are normally the responsibility of the executive management team led by the CEO. There are too many factors to consider to expect the CEO to be the only individual who makes the investment decisions. The CEO's role here is one of leader and coordinator. They ensure that the focus is on the strategic goals and various priorities of the different parts of the organization in the context of the strategic goals. Once investment decisions are made, balancing technology investments against investments elsewhere using consistent measures such as ROI, the CEO must communicate a consistent understanding of the organization's plan to the entire organization.

Throughout the remainder of the VRC of cultivating to produce an asset, nurturing to produce an impact, and harvesting to produce business value, the CEO plays the highest role at the governance level. It is unlikely that it is appropriate for the CEO to participate in the details of any particular project. This does not mean that he or she does not get regular updates. However, other levels of governance should be acting to make sure that the project is either on track to deliver effective results or canceled because it is no longer capable of doing so.

After the harvest—the business value being produced by application of the new asset—is recognized and accounted for, the CEO reenters the VRC as an active player. Assessing the impact on the strategic objectives and making any changes to the strategy is an area where the CEO's leadership is necessary. Any resulting changes to the strategy must be effectively communicated and again the CEO plays a key role here.

Beyond the VRC, the CEO has a responsibility to support and develop the CIO. This is the case whether the CIO reports to the CEO or elsewhere in the organization. If CIOs are to be effective organizational leaders, then they must be in sync with the CEO. If they are not and conflicting messages are delivered, the chance to realize value from investments or from existing systems is severely reduced. The CEO should be sure that the CIO has a complete and thorough understanding of the business objectives of the organization and its strategy.

The CFO's Role in the Value Realization Cycle

Like CIOs, CFOs have two roles. They are corporate leaders focused on financial assets and employment of these assets across the entire organization. They are also the leaders of the finance department. As such, the CIO and the CFO are natural allies, regardless of the reporting structure of the organization.

Like the CIO, the CFO needs a clearly understood and consistent strategy to be in place. Where the CIO is concerned about the role that technology plays in achieving this strategy, the CFO is focused on the financial aspects. How much money is being spent when and where, and with what results? The CFO should be as adamant, or more adamant, than anyone else as to the need to clearly measure both costs and returns for the full extent of any existing system or new project. For example, if a system is intended to deliver a reduction in costs, the CFO should insist on understanding exactly which line in whose budget is going to be reduced by what amount.

The CFO will want to ensure that they understand all the costs involved in an investment, not just the project expenses. Figure 12.1 shows the scope that the CFO and other leaders should consider for fully loaded costs of the VRC.

The CFO has an important role to play in the strategy phase of the VRC. This is focused largely on measurement of outcomes and on ensuring that the organization is being realistic in its spending intent. In public companies, this will also likely include the impact on shareholders and share price. In government organizations, this will have a strong influence on alignment with political goals of elected representatives. In nonprofits, the focus of the CFO will be on ensuring alignment with the donors. In other words, the CFO is key to making sure that the Value Cycle is understood in the context of the individual at the center of the Value Cycle.

Organizations often can have eyes bigger than their stomachs—they wish to achieve many things, but when these are added together, it is more than the organization can reasonably be expected to accomplish. The CFO's first objective will be to view the portfolio of planned activities in terms of the financial resources of the organization. Many CFOs will also be the ones that best understands the non-financial resources of the organization. The CFO is in the strongest position to enforce a level of discipline on the executive management team as investment decisions are being made.

Once investment decisions have been made the CFO, like the CEO, steps back and plays a role at the senior level of governance through the next phases of the VRC. The exception to this would be a project or system focused on the finance organization wherein the CFO must play the role as department head as well as organizational leader. In that situation, the CFO will also be a business leader, as described later in this chapter.

Once the harvest of business value from the investment is now recognized and accounted for, the CFO should now play a strong role in considering how well that harvest matched the intentions of the investment decisions. They are in a particularly good position to act as arbitrator in any disputes and ensure that a realistic and objective assessment of any system is undertaken. It is at this point that CFOs may often wish to do an audit of a system or group of systems. This is further described later in this chapter under the auditor role.

With a realistic assessment of the new business value, the CFO, as a leader within the governance structure at the highest level, should take a lead in assessing the impact on the strategy of the new situation. Completing the

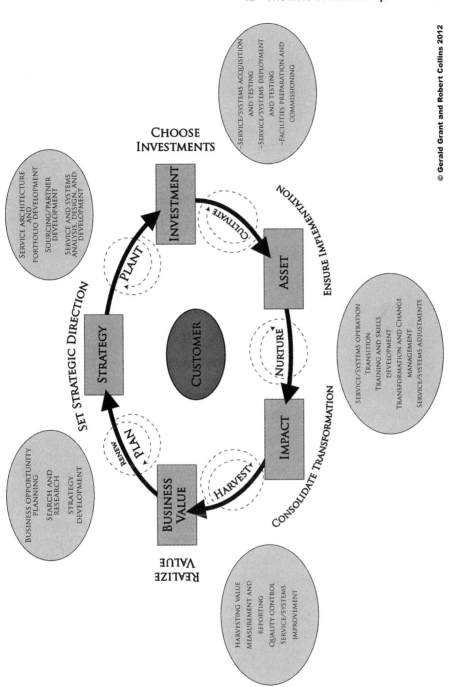

Fig. 12.1 Fully loaded costs in the VRC

renewal phase to adjust the strategy is a priority that the CFO along with the CEO are in the best position to enforce.

The CFO and IT

It was stated above that the CIO and the CFO are natural allies. Yet, we have often found that this relationship is one of friction rather than collaboration. We believe, in large part, that this stems from the tendency of CIOs and IT departments to discuss technology when the CFO is worried about ROI, risk, and cost control. In speaking with CFOs and other financial leaders in the public and private sector, we have identified a number of questions that the CIO must address to develop this relationship into a mutually productive partnership.

- What is this large and growing expense (the IT budget) and can it be curtailed?
- How can I judge the value of IT investments?
- Is IT managing risk responsibly?
- Does IT really understand the cost and effort required to realize value from technology investments?

The IT budget is often a very significant portion of an organization's spending. When the value realized from IT is being challenged, this budget looms large in the CFO's mind as a place where cuts can be made. When IT fails to communicate value effectively, it raises questions. Growing costs, such as continuing maintenance fees, software and hardware upgrades, and additional user fees, all give the appearance that IT's budget is growing out of control.

CIOs who do not address the questions that CFOs carry in their minds run a serious risk of losing the support of the CFO. When an organization comes under economic pressure, it has to react quickly. The CFO is often the driver of such reaction. Under such circumstances, CIOs may find the entire IT department outsourced before they can establish its value to the organization.

This potentially drastic action can effectively be managed by the CIO communicating the value of everything in the IT farm. That can be a daunting task when there is a large legacy of technology in an organization. To do so requires effort to produce portfolios and enterprise architectures (EAs). The CIO can start by coordinating a value audit (see auditors role below) on some manageable portion (or portfolio) of the IT farm. Having an external (i.e., not IT) assessor investigate and detail the costs and benefits of the IT portfolio will give both the CFO and the CIO a basis for a discussion that can overcome the generic concerns harbored by many CFOs.

The Business Unit Leader in the VRC

Leaders of all departments within the organization enter the VRC at the strategic level. They could be heads of Sales, HR, Support, Manufacturing, or other departments. As part of the executive management team under the leadership of the CEO, they must participate in developing the strategy and must buy in to the final result. They must effectively communicate that strategy to their organizations in coordination with the corporate efforts of the CEO.

These business unit leaders most seriously affect the VRC with regards to the decisions as to which investments are to be made. It is natural that they will always be torn between the ultimate good of the overall organization and the specific needs of their various departments. They must fight to get the necessary support needed by their individual functions. However, it is rarely possible for every department to get everything they need. They must participate in the give-and-take of an organization with limited resources. Once decisions have been made, they must communicate not only which investments will be undertaken but also which investments will not be undertaken at the current time.

Business unit leaders must assign the necessary staff to participate in project. This includes those who will actively partake in the development of new systems as well as the appropriate individuals to participate at the various levels of governance. Of course the business leaders themselves are part of that governance structure at the higher levels. Like the CxOs, business unit leaders must clearly communicate the harvest expected and keep the focus on that harvest. They cannot allow themselves to be dragged down into the details and lose that focus.

During the planting and cultivation phases that produce an asset intended to be used by their departments, the business unit leaders must ensure that the right people are participating effectively in the project. These executives need to ensure that they are receiving regular updates on the progress of any project as part of the governance process. Too often business leaders find that they are surprised by sudden changes to systems or projects. They can reduce the likelihood of such shocks by ensuring that they are active participants in governance.

In the nurturing phase, to make sure that a new asset is having an impact on the business processes, the business unit leaders are the primary executives responsible for delivering results. Supported by IT and possibly other departments, these business units must drive the effort to ensure the maximum harvest. The executive in charge will need to play a more active role during this phase — encouraging their teams, ensuring that the focus remains on the harvest, and that an effective "weather eye" is being applied to the effort.

The resulting harvest will be the work of the business unit applying the new assets. The measurement of that harvest is the responsibility of that business unit and ultimately its senior executive. This implies that during the nurturing and cultivation phases, the business unit must stress the need to build measurement into the asset and the processes. The communication of the resulting harvest at the highest levels of governance is the responsibility of the business unit leader.

During the renewal phase, the business unit leader, supported by the CIO, must communicate to the executive team the realized value and ultimate impact of the changes made in any project or system. They should be communicating the implications of this impact on the strategic goals as set out in the organizational strategy. Then, along with the impact of other investments, the executive management team must assess the strategy overall.

The Role of the Auditor

It can be challenging to assess the impact and status of projects and systems. Even with clearly defined measurements, the value achieved may be disputed. It is in this circumstance that an auditor, especially an internal auditor, can play an extremely effective role. An auditor brings a more objective stance to the assessment of any project or system at any point in the VRC.

The obvious place for an internal auditor to be introduced into the VRC is during the renewal phase. With the realized business value in hand and the bulk of the expenses of creating or maintaining a new asset accounted for, an auditor can assess the impact relative to the goals that made an investment decision necessary. However, it can be more effective to include the internal auditor at the very beginning of the process—where investment decisions are being made. This can facilitate early identification of issues to be addressed and will allow the auditor to explain how the effort will be audited, thus avoiding confusion and confrontation at the end of the cycle.

During the planting phase, with the targeted ROI clearly stated in the investment decision, an internal auditor can identify at the beginning of a project what assessments will be made when the initial harvest is eventually realized. This clearly defined set of rules can be extremely effective in keeping disparate teams focused on the goals of the harvest. Knowing how they will be assessed after the project is complete can avoid the traps of scope creep and defocusing. It can also prevent recriminations and difficulties at the end of the project. But most importantly, it improves the chances that the maximum business value will be realized.

Auditors, be they internal or external, should not focus solely on the latter stages of the VRC. An audit should start with the strategy where the VRC starts. If the strategy does not effectively communicate the results needed, then it is difficult for any investment to succeed. Should this be the case, it is important that an audit identify this early problem, as it may be the root of any other problems realized later. The auditor should assess each phase of the Value Realization Cycle and report on the results of those as part of the investment review (Fig. 12.2).

Audits should not be restricted solely to new investments. A critical factor for many organizations is the amount of resources, human and capital, that are necessary to maintain the existing portfolio of systems. An audit of such a portfolio is often the most effective means of performing the renewal phase of the entire IT farm or some significant portion thereof. Such an audit can have a significant impact on strategy in order to reduce ineffective assets and processes and free up resources to be applied to new investments.

An audit is also the easiest point to introduce the new concepts of the Agricultural Model, the Value Cycle, and the VRC to an organization. By selecting one system or project and doing an audit on it, an organization can assess what they lacked by not having the VRC in place and not addressing the various components of the Agricultural Model. This can be the easiest way to convince an organization to change from the ineffective engineering model that has been failing it and move to the Agricultural Model. We strongly recommend this as the starting point for any organization looking to improve the value that they achieve from their investments in IT.

Leadership

An organization is effective only if the leaders of the organization and its various functions operate as a team. Each member of the senior team has a role, or roles, to play in any investment or the ongoing maintenance of existing systems in the IT farm.

This can only occur if there is a clear organizational strategy that is communicable in a measurable fashion. It is essential that the strategy and its measures are communicated at all levels and in all departments of the organization. The CxOs can play a strong role in supporting this well beyond the limits of the IT or finance department but must be working in cooperation with the other organizational leaders.

Investment decisions resulting from the strategy are the responsibility of all leaders of the organization. Those in the CxO positions have a vested

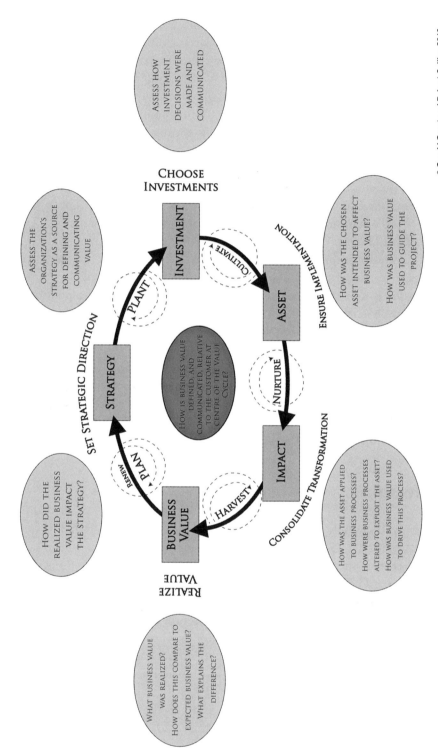

Fig. 12.2   Using the VRC to audit returns from IT investments

interest ensuring that this responsibility is being effectively addressed across the organization. This is possible only when an effective governance regime is put in place and maintained, not only for new and special projects but on an ongoing basis.

Whether it is new investments or existing assets, the business value harvest—must be assessed on a regular basis. This assessment must be done by the organizations whose business processes deliver that business value. They are supported by the IT department which delivers and maintains the assets that support these business processes. This ongoing assessment is the renewal phase that must be undertaken at least annually to ensure that the money being spent in the IT and the business units applying the technology is returning the expected harvest. Where it is not, it is necessary to adjust the strategy to address the issues uncovered.

As discussed earlier, an internal audit can be the most effective way of introducing these concepts to an organization. Such an audit goes beyond the political factors and personalities involved in any organization and delivers concrete data to drive strategic objectives. It will also identify issues of governance that may be preventing an organization from realizing the potential of their IT investments.

Only when leaders of the organization understand their role in the VRC and play those roles effectively can organizations truly obtain the maximum benefit promised by the myriad of technology available today.

Discussion Questions

1. Who are the leaders in your organization that need to participate in the VRC?
2. What role do the CEO, CFO, and CIO (or equivalents) play in your organization today?
3. What role do business unit leaders play in delivering and assessing business value through the application of IT today?
4. What changes need to occur in your organization to effectively implement the Agricultural Model and the VRC?

13

It's Not About Technology: It's About Value

The promise that information technology (IT) holds is immense. The Internet, social media, big data, the cloud, and many other technologies offer almost unlimited potential if we can effectively harness them. They can truly transform our organizations and our world. At the same time, they present us with challenges that range from security to increased expectations. Any organization that is not focusing on how to apply such technology risks becoming irrelevant or fatally uncompetitive in the next few years.

Yet we are always playing catch up. In the time it takes to implement these technologies, the technologies themselves change. As new technologies are deployed, some will become fundamental while others will prove a disappointment. The IT industry is all about change—the change in the technology and the change it can bring to our organizations.

In spite of that, the basic understanding of how IT departments do their job has not embraced that change. IT departments continue to be isolated from their organizations. Business leaders express constant frustration that they are not getting what they need from IT while CFOs despair at the money that is spent without achieving expected returns. If we are going to achieve the promise of transformation via IT, we are going to have to change the basic model with which we understand how to effectively deliver value for investing in IT.

We must, throughout the organization, stop focusing primarily on technology and schedules. Instead, we must focus on creating value. The technology is the means to do this; and schedules are vital to understand how, when, and if we are going to invest. But technology and schedules are not the goal.

© The Editor(s) (if applicable) and The Author(s) 2016
G.G. Grant, R. Collins, *The Value Imperative*,
DOI 10.1057/978-1-137-59040-4_13

Business value is the goal. If you take nothing else away from reading this book, take to heart the mantra—Focus on the harvest!

The harvest of business value is the very basis of alignment between the IT department and all other departments in the organization. It is the direct tie to strategy and organization goals. It is the universal language that crosses all boundaries. It is the primary basis of all major decisions. It is the final arbiter of success. We firmly believe that an IT organization can only succeed when it can clearly communicate the business value of its work and its potential investments.

The Value Cycle

To be able to communicate business value, it is necessary to have an understanding of the target of that value and the effort to create it. The Value Cycle, as described in Chap. 2, is something every organization must have and must communicate throughout that organization. Who is at the center of your Value Cycle? How do they describe the value they seek? This is the language that must be used to assess value creation—not the language of the computer room.

Articulating value is not solely the responsibility of the IT department but it is a vital tool for that department. By communicating in the language of the organization (or the organization's customer), IT ensures that it is making a real connection with other departments. This is the basis of alignment that has so long been sought and so rarely achieved. This is also the basis for assessment of existing systems as well as future investments. It is a means to compare different implementation options and different IT investments. It is also a way to compare IT investments with nontechnical investments across the organization.

Business value, as created by the Value Cycle and expressed in terms of the individual at the center of that cycle, is the only valid measure of success of any IT (or even non-IT) project or system.

The Engineering Model

As noted above, IT has the potential to bring about transformational change. It is astounding then, that we approach that change using a model that treats change as error. The Engineering Model, which assumes that all things can be known in advance, is a mirage that has played us all false for decades. Its focus on the schedule and technology features causes organizations to look away from the business value that should be the primary purpose of their efforts.

In Chap. 3, we outlined how this model has failed organizations. The Engineering Model is fundamentally disconnected from business value and the Value Cycle. It is a proven failure, and we must consign it to the scrap heap of failed ideas if we are to succeed in transforming organizations through IT.

The Agricultural Model

So what do we put in place of the Engineering Model? In Chap. 4, we introduced the Agricultural Model. Unlike the Engineering Model, the Agricultural Model focuses primarily on business value—the *harvest*. Rather than blindly rejecting change, with the Agricultural Model we use a "weather eye" to seek out change and address it early and effectively. This model does not reject schedules, budgets, and good methodologies. Rather, it embraces them and places them within a framework that puts business value at the heart of all decisions.

Where the Engineering Model focuses solely on the creation of an asset, the Agricultural Model covers all aspects needed to successfully deliver business value from IT systems. It does not start with the project or system. It starts with organizational strategy. Based on the objectives of the organization and the measurable value to be created, a decision is made to implement a technology to achieve a result. This is the planting phase—the first step toward achieving business value.

That technology must be honed to achieve the business value expected. This effort is cultivation. Rather than just dump the system on the user communities, it is fine-tuned to work with the business processes with an eye always on the harvest. This cannot be done by IT alone but must involve the rest of the organization. This ensures that the technology is right for the organization.

Just as important is the effort by the departments using the technology to prepare and adjust to exploit that technology. Led by the user community and supported by IT, business processes are changed to ensure the value can be created. This is the nurturing phase of the Agricultural Model. Users, and even customers, are educated as to the goals and processes that exploit the new technology, thus ensuring that the organization is prepared to exploit the potential of the technology.

With this, all the requirements are in place to create value. But we cannot assume that value creation just happens. As discussed in Chap. 4, value can be appropriated away from the intended goals. The realized value is not always the intended value. That is why the production of value must be actively sought to deliver the harvest. It is here that value is measured to ensure that the intentions of the investment are turned into real returns. The harvest is actual, measurable business value.

Even after the harvest, which occurs on a regular basis, the Agricultural Model tells us that our work is not done. We must look to the broad IT farm to understand how it has changed as a result of the new crop just harvested. What threatens future harvests? What other opportunities exist that should be considered? This information has to be cycled back into the strategy from which we started. This is the renewal phase. Its results are strategic plans that are adjusted to take into account the impact of past investments and future change.

The Agricultural Model embraces all phases of the effort to turn an investment into real business value through the implementation and exploitation of information technology.

The Value Realization Cycle (VRC)

The Agricultural Model is best viewed within the Value Realization Cycle (VRC), as described in Chap. 5. This cycle starts with the organizational strategy. From there, decisions are made about planting that result in an **investment**. The investment is then adapted to the organization during the cultivation phase. The results of this are an **asset**. The asset, on its own, does not deliver the real business value sought. That can only occur when the asset is applied to the organization's business processes. To do this, nurturing of the business processes and affected departments must occur. This means applying the asset through different business processes that have an **impact** on the organization. This impact is then harvested and produces **business value.**

The results of these changes, along with other systems and environmental issues are then fed back into the strategy via the planning process. This affects the strategy and the cycle continues.

It is vital to understand that business value is not created by IT. It does not come from the assets that they deliver. Rather it is created by other parts of the organization who apply those assets to their altered business processes. It is the impact of this change that is harvested as business value. This important realization should be reflected in the relationship of IT to the rest of the organization and in the understanding of who is accountable for achieving business value. It is the user departments that are accountable, and therefore, who must be the primary drivers of such investments. IT's role is in support of these departments, acquiring, adapting, and supporting technology to help them achieve the business result.

Governance

This understanding of responsibilities and relationships leads directly to the vital role of governance. Governance creates a framework for decision making about what opportunities and strategies to pursue, who should be involved and in what ways, what investments should be made, and how the process of value creation and delivery are monitored and measured. As outlined in Chap. 6, governance occurs at different levels and in different areas but is all connected into a single governance framework. It involves IT and non-IT functions and deals with projects as well as ongoing business processes. It stretches from the boardroom to the computer room.

Without a proper governance structure, we argue that no organization can deliver business value on an ongoing basis.

Communication Tools

Governance cannot occur without effective communication, and effective communication is not possible without a common and realistic understanding of the organization and its technology. While this communication must be based on business value, it must also include an understanding of how the larger IT platform affects the delivery of that value. It must deal with the whole picture and not just focus on isolated aspects of the environment in which they exist.

In Chap. 7, we talked about enterprise architecture (EA) as a vital communication tool. The EA provides a picture that starts with the business value and the processes that produce it. It then drills down through the data, applications, technology, and facilities. By showing the relationship between these various layers as well as the various items within each layer, an EA makes it possible to understand how business decisions affect technology and vice versa. This is essential to translating business issues into technology discussions and technology challenges into business impacts.

In Chap. 8, we discussed the idea of portfolio management. Like an investment portfolio, the IT portfolio consists of a number of systems (investments) that are producing their individual returns. Different views of the portfolio can highlight different aspects of the organization and the technology. By using these different views, the organizational and technical challenges can be kept in perspective. Portfolio management provides a simple, yet powerful, means to view the complex environment by highlighting specific technical factors and communicating their impact on business value.

EA and portfolio management are not the only tools that can be used. We have highlighted these because we have experienced their success in many organizations. They provide a solid foundation for governance and for investment decisions.

Sourcing

Too often, sourcing decisions are made as a result of the frustrations brought about by the failed relationship between IT and the rest of the organization. When this occurs, drastic measures can be taken that have far-reaching and potentially seriously negative repercussions. In Chap. 9, we argued that all sourcing options are worthy of consideration and that a mix of sourcing solutions is almost always the right answer.

Sourcing decisions must be made in context of the VRC with an understanding of their impact on the Value Cycle. This can easily be done when a good governance structure is in place, supported by effective communication tools such as EA and portfolio management. In fact, a portfolio view focused on sourcing options can be a useful part of the annual governance review (the renewal phase).

Measurement

We strongly agree with the old adage "You cannot manage what you cannot measure". However, many organizations struggle with the measurement of their IT portfolio. This is often brought about by a focus on technology rather than on the harvest. All measurement should be based on business value as articulated by the individual at the center of the Value Cycle. Only then can an organization truly assess if an investment is worth making or an existing system worth maintaining.

While fiscal measurements are most common and most easily managed, they are not appropriate for all organizations or circumstances. However, the lack of a fiscal outcome is not an excuse not to measure. As explained in Chap. 10, there are many ways to measure less objective outcomes that can still provide the means to assess value creation.

These are best embodied in the idea of return on investment (ROI). This concept was discussed at length in Chap. 11. ROI provides a common means to compare different investments (or existing systems). It should be the basis of decision making when translating strategy into investment. Through ROI, it is possible to assess different alternatives for addressing a specific investment as well as different investments. By ensuring that ROI is communicated in business value terms, it is also possible to assess IT investments against investments in other areas of the organization.

ROI, and other measures, provide that basis for assessing the success or failure of any project or existing system. Assessing expected and realized ROI over time from the beginning of the planting phase through the regular renewal phase is the very basis of good IT governance. It is also the best means possible to recognize when a project should be stopped because it will no longer deliver the expected result and to do so as early as possible to ensure the best use of scarce resources.

Leadership

Moving from the Engineering Model and its failures to the Agricultural Model and its acknowledgement of the complexities and business realities requires leadership. We believe that the chief information officer (CIO) can make no greater contribution to an organization than to make this transition. This must happen both within the IT department and in the organization as a whole. That is why, as discussed in Chap. 12, we see the CIO as having two complementary and demanding roles. The first is to be the leader to the IT department. The latter is to be a leader of the entire organization.

It is not possible for IT to do this alone. The focus on strategy and business value, and the recognition that it is the user departments who create that value, requires that change come from the leadership of the organization outside of IT. Every member of the executive team has a role to play in the VRC. The CIO can facilitate that leadership and bring the organization along in making the transition.

Embracing the Agricultural Model

So how does one go about making such a change? Despite all its failures, we have been working with the Engineering Model for a long time. It is comfortable even as it is unsuccessful. The CIO must guide the organization away from this familiar mirage. To do that, there must be adroit management and purposeful leadership.

A good first step is to actively recognize and communicate the problem. This could be in the form of a value audit of some part of the IT portfolio. Take the time to understand what value that existing systems and investments are producing and how well that fits with the goals of the organization as a whole. In doing so, the CIO may find that they are spending more time getting the organization to clarify its goals, strategy, and measures than worrying about how IT can contribute. That is fine. If these things are not commonly understood and easily communicable, then there is no hope for IT to contribute to real business value.

This cannot come solely from IT. The chief financial officer (CFO) is a likely ally in understanding the challenge and hitting the reset button on IT's relationship with the rest of the organization. As the person most likely to be worried about business value and shareholder, donor, or citizen returns, they should be easy to engage in a review of the existing situation. It will also be necessary to enlist the effort and time of organizational leaders outside IT and Finance.

The Harvest Creates Alignment

By moving to the Agricultural Model, the CIO can create real and lasting alignment with the rest of the organization. This is not the false alignment created in the Engineering Model to serve the purposes of a single project. This is deep and enduring alignment based on organizational goals that naturally brings disparate parts of the organization together. This is the holy grail of IT departments and has been for over a decade. Having this lasting alignment will allow the CIO to ensure that IT is focused on efforts that produce real value for the person at the center of the Value Cycle. The corollary of that is the elimination of efforts that are not contributing, as well as elimination of the churn of priorities that is the bane of every IT leader.

The focus on business value allows the CIO to demonstrate proof of IT's contribution to the organization using measures that make sense to the whole organization and to those outside (such as the customer or taxpayer). The inability to explicitly state IT's value in a meaningful way is, we believe, the major factor in the budget and investment constraints that hold back organizations today.

The common language of the Value Cycle and the harvest make it possible for the CIO to engage the rest of the organization to make the hard decisions. When people don't understand what IT is really doing, it is easy to blame IT for not doing the right things. When organizational leadership understands how initiatives are tied to strategy and have measurable outcomes to assess, it falls to the organization as a whole to make the decisions as to where to invest. This is then backed up by a governance structure that, using business value, keeps the priorities consistent and focused.

IT's Goals Are the Organization's Goals

CFOs want to increase ROI, understand the value of efforts, and reduce risk. The Agricultural Model speaks directly to all of these. It requires that a measurable expected value (ROI) be identified for all potential investments. Similarly, it provides for the assessment of business value contribution of all existing systems that can be compared to their cost and effort. These allow the organization to make business decisions rather than technical decisions as to which efforts to fund, which to defer, and which to eliminate.

The use of ROI also brings IT into the mainstream of the organization. Having ROI for IT projects as well as for non-IT investments gives the organization the ability to make holistic business decisions rather than treating IT as a special breed of investment.

With these types of measures, IT investments can now be clearly tied to organizational strategy. This makes it easy to eliminate pet projects whose value is not tied to those strategic goals. This ensures that the limited investment funds are being spent on the right efforts.

Finally, focusing on business value throughout the life cycle of any technology makes it easy to shut down efforts that are not returning value. That is the best reduction of risk that can be sought. With an understanding that failures will not be pursued to completion as they are in the Engineering Model, it is easier for Finance to approve investment knowing that risk is being managed.

Not all departmental leaders have the broad view that is expected of the CFO and CIO. They have their own departments to manage and they need to know what's in it for them. This is especially true when the responsibility for delivering value is correctly laid at their door rather than at IT's.

One of the biggest complaints of these leaders is that they cannot influence plans as to what IT will deliver. In most organizations today, business leaders find IT an opaque organization that makes decisions in a vacuum that does not give them predictability. The Agricultural Model changes that. By making investment decisions based on business value rather than who yells loudest (or was the last to yell) or which technologies seem coolest, the levers to affect IT's priorities are clearly in their hands.

Decisions based on organizational strategy and business value, supported by a governance process in which these departments participate, addresses lack of predictability. This is the other major complaint that line-of-business leaders have about IT. When the decisions as to what is and what is not to be implemented are clearly and broadly communicated in context of organizational strategy, they can plan with the full knowledge necessary and know that it will not suddenly change. Even if their preferred project is not approved, they at least know this and can account for it in their business plans.

While the Agricultural Model does not promise every departmental leader that their pet project will get done, it does promise to produce fewer failures and fewer surprises. That, alone, is often very attractive to business leaders who feel IT is a black box full of uncertainty.

Communication and Training

All of this is going to take a lot of communication. The CIO is going to need to communicate inside and outside IT about what is happening, why it is happening, and what value can be expected. As with any communication plan, it will require a consistent message that is repeated regularly.

This effort should be supported by training that is focused specifically on the Agricultural Model. By taking the time to understand what it is and what it offers, people can be persuaded to embrace it. And it is important that they embrace it, not just acknowledge it. After all, the participation of the entire organization is needed to make IT investment successful.

Good training can best be focused on specific, real-world issues that exist within the organization and are not just generic, out-of-the-box slide decks. The goal is significant change, and people need to understand it in the context of their roles and their problems. They need to be able to ask questions and have discussions, not just listen to speeches.

The Value Audit

Doing a value audit of an organization, as referenced earlier, can be especially effective. Looking at where IT is spending its effort and the associated value produced by those efforts can be highly enlightening (and often quite scary). A value audit would also include an assessment of efforts and investments relative to stated organizational strategy. Again, this can starkly illustrate where IT's efforts are, and aren't, contributing to the success of the organization.

Value audits do not focus on technology. They are not the traditional IT review of whether the latest or greatest technologies are being used or how well the IT infrastructure is tied together. While that is very useful information (and should be part of any good EA), it does not address the primary question—How is IT contributing to measurable business value that is aligned with organizational strategy?

A value audit can bring the whole discussion of IT's performance out of the weeds of day-to-day issues and refocus it on the highest-level priorities of the organization. It makes the perfect starting point for repositioning IT as a contributor to value that is well-integrated into the organization rather than a group of techies that speak another language.

It is not always possible for value audits to be done effectively by people within the organization. Such efforts often fall prey to existing prejudices, relationships, and patterns. It is difficult for a CIO who has been in the role for several years to try to start fresh. We have found that bringing in an outsider with credible expertise but without direct experience of the particular organization can be most effective. Such individuals can more easily penetrate to the core issues because they can justifiably ask the difficult questions and more easily challenge conventional wisdom.

Mentoring

Throughout this process, we have found that mentoring can play an excellent role in helping bring about change. This mentoring can be most effective when it brings in outside expertise. Having access to individuals who have gone through the process to advise and discuss throughout the shift to the Agricultural Model significantly enhances the chance of success.

Mentoring within the organization can also help advance the organization. By having business people mentor key IT staff on the business processes and measures, and conversely having IT mentor business on the potential value and pitfalls of technology, an organization not only gets staff better educated to move through the process of value realization, but also builds the relationships that are often lacking between technical and nontechnical areas. This mentoring can be extended right down through the organization.

Conclusion

We believe that applying the Agricultural Model with a good understanding of the Value Cycle and VRC can make it possible for any organization to effectively apply IT to transform that organization. Further, we argue that organizations that do not shift away from the mirage of the Engineering Model are doomed to failure, technologically in the short run and for the organization as a whole in the long run.

Be it businesses, governments, charities, nonprofits, or educational institutions, organizations must answer to individuals who provide the money that allows them to carry out their mission. More and more, these individuals, whom we see at the center of the Value Cycle, assess organizations on how well they employ technology to achieve their goals. But they do not measure technology, they measure value, be it profitability, service delivery, or amelioration of social issues. And they measure it in their own terms. Those organizations that do not change their thinking to focus on that business value in the way they apply technology will not last long into the twenty-first century. To be successful and to thrive, organizations must focus on the *harvest*.

Index

Printed in the United States of America